THE   BOOK   OF

Crêpes & Omelettes

THE BOOK OF

Crêpes & Omelettes

MARY NORWAK

Photography by
JON STEWART

TED SMART

Specially produced for Ted Smart,
Guardian House, Borough Road,
Godalming, Surrey GU7 2AE

By arrangement with Merehurst Press,
51/57 Lacy Road, Putney, London SW15 1PR

ISBN: 1 85613 9204

Managing Editor: Felicity Jackson
Editor: Beverly LeBlanc
Designer: Roger Daniels
Home Economist: Sarah Bush
Photographer: Jon Stewart, assisted by Alistair Thorpe
Typeset by AKM Associates (UK) Ltd, Southall, London
Colour separation by J. Film Process Ltd, Bangkok, Thailand
Printed in Belgium by Proost International Book Production

ACKNOWLEDGEMENTS

The publishers would like to thank the following for their
help and advice:

David Mellor, 26 James Street, Covent Garden, London WC2 8PA,
4 Sloane Square, London SW1 8EE and
66 King Street, Manchester M2 4NP

CONTENTS

INTRODUCTION

Crêpes and omelettes are universal dishes. These simple egg mixtures are quickly prepared and cooked to produce many delectable dishes, and nearly every country in the world has its own variations. Once the basic techniques are mastered, crêpes and omelettes can be served at every meal of the day, for fillings and flavourings can vary from the most simple to the very sophisticated and savoury to sweet.

A crêpe is a mixture of flour, eggs and liquid cooked over high heat to lacy fineness. Variations include thick puffy pancakes made from different grains, and each country has its own favourite toppings, ranging from caviar and thick sour cream, through smoked fish, vegetables, meat and fruit, and a huge range of sweet-tooth favourites. Crêpes may be folded, rolled or formed into parcels, and coated in sauces — the variety is endless.

Waffles, also included in this book, like crêpes, are made from a flour, egg and liquid batter, but cooked in a waffle iron. Baking powder in the batter makes them light and puffy. Sweet or savoury flavourings can be added to the batter, or the waffle may be plain with a variety of toppings. Always follow the manufacturer's instructions when using a waffle iron.

An omelette is an even more simple dish of eggs, butter and flavourings, but many people have not mastered the basic technique of preparation and serving. In this book there are easy to follow step-by-step instructions for the perfect golden omelette and its many savoury and sweet variations. Here are the answers for producing the most delicious snack as well as main courses and desserts which represent a triumph for any cook.

EQUIPMENT

The correct pan is the most important piece of equipment for making crêpes and omelettes. Other equipment consists of common kitchen equipment, such as bowls, and forks.

Crêpe and Omelette Pan

The pan may be made of cast iron or aluminium, or may be finished with a non-stick surface. It should be approximately 5 cm (2 in) deep, with a thick base and curved sides. A 17.5 cm (7 in) pan is most useful for crêpes and 3-egg omelettes, and a 20–22.5 cm (8–9 in) pan is best for 5–6 egg omelettes. A 10 cm (4 in) pan is useful for Half Moon Omelettes, see page 110.

The pan should be kept exclusively for crêpes and omelettes, as it is important to keep the surface smooth so that the delicate mixtures do not stick.

Proving a Pan

All new pans, except the non-stick type, must be 'proved' before use. This means creating a surface to which eggs will not stick, and which will remain smooth while cooking a batch of crêpes or omelettes. Old pans which tend to stick may also be 'proved'. There are two good ways of doing this:

1. Cover the base of the pan with 1 cm (½ in) cooking salt, put over low heat and leave for 30 minutes, until hot. Remove from heat and

rub hard with a ball of absorbent kitchen paper, then leave until cool and wipe with a dry cloth.

2. Cover the base of the pan with 1 cm (½ in) olive oil and heat very gently for 5 minutes, then remove from heat and leave to stand for at least 12 hours. Pour off the oil and wipe the pan's surface with absorbent kitchen paper.

Care and Storage
A pan used for crêpes and omelettes should not be washed. After use, the pan should be wiped with kitchen paper and stored in a polythene bag.

If a pan begins to stick when in use, do not wash, but, instead, repeat one of the 'proving' processes.

Other Equipment
The equipment listed below is useful for making crêpes and omelettes, and all the items are easily available. *A small saucepan* may be needed for preparing fillings.

Weighing scales (or cup measure) are used for dry ingredients and fats.

A large bowl is useful for mixing to incorporate lots of air.

Measuring spoons (a tablespoon and teaspoon) are needed for small quantities of ingredients.

A large fork or straight-edged non-metal spatula is needed for omelette-making, to draw liquid egg from the sides to centre of pan.

A flexible palette knife is needed to turn crêpes, and to fold omelettes, and to lift them onto serving dishes.

CRÊPE TECHNIQUES

The best crepes are thin, light and lacy, and indeed almost transparent, and they may be served with a simple spread or other flavouring, or used as a packaging for substantial fillings. A similar batter mixture lightened by a raising agent, such as baking powder or yeast, may be cooked as small thick puffy pancakes to be served with a variety of toppings.

Ingredients

Crêpe batter is made with flour from wheat or other grains mixed with milk and eggs. A thin layer of this mixture is fried in a heavy-based pan lightly greased with vegetable oil or lard. If a very light crisp crêpe is required, a little melted butter or flavourless oil, such as corn oil, may be added to the batter before cooking.

Basic Preparation

To make the batter, sift the flour and salt into a bowl, make a well in the centre and add the eggs and a little milk. Beat with a wooden spoon, gradually drawing in flour from the edge of the bowl. As the mixture thickens, gradually add half the milk, beating well until smooth, then add remaining milk, beating hard until bubbling on top. All the ingredients may also be blended together at once in a blender or food processor until smooth and bubbling.

There is no need to leave the batter to stand before using. If left to stand, it will thicken, and a little more milk will be needed before use. The batter should be like thin cream to make light crêpes.

Heat just enough vegetable oil or lard in a crêpe pan to cover the base. When a slight haze rises, pour in 6–9 teaspoons batter to thinly cover the base of the pan; tilt the pan quickly so the base is evenly covered with batter. Cook for about 1 minute, until lightly browned underneath, then quickly turn the crêpe over with a palette knife and cook

the other side for 30 seconds. Lift out onto a warm plate, keep warm in a low oven and continue cooking crêpes until all the batter has been used.

Fillings and Sauces

Crêpes may be spread with jam, honey, fruit purée or citrus juice and sugar. If the filling is slightly warmed, it will spread more easily without tearing the crêpes. More substantial fillings are chopped fruit or ice cream for the sweet course. Savoury fillings may be meat, fish, poultry, cheese or vegetables, mixed with sauce, yogurt or cream. Filled crêpes may be covered in a cheese sauce and flashed under the grill or put in the oven to brown.

Storing and Reheating

Crêpes are best when freshly cooked. To keep a batch warm for immediate use, place the crêpes in a stack in a low oven, or on a heat-proof plate over a pan of boiling water.

Crêpes may be prepared in advance and stored in a refrigerator for 5–6 days. They should be stacked and wrapped in foil or a polythene bag. They may be quickly reheated by cooking in a lightly greased pan for 30 seconds on each side. Alternatively, the cold crêpes may be wrapped round a filling and heated in the oven.

Freezing and Thawing

Stack cold crêpes with interleaving sheets of greaseproof paper, or polythene, then wrap tightly in foil or a freezer bag, label and freeze for up to 6 months.

To use the crêpes, thaw at room temperature for 3 hours, or overnight in a refrigerator. For speed, spread out crêpes in a single layer and thaw at room temperature for 15 minutes.

If preferred, remove interleaving and stack 4–6 crêpes, wrap in foil and heat in oven at 200C (400F/Gas 6) for 25 minutes.

FOLDING AND SERVING CRÊPES

The versatile crêpe can be served in many ways. Serve flat crêpes with the topping arranged pizza-style. Or spread with a simple filling, such as jam or lemon juice and sugar, and fold 2 or 3 times to give a long, flat roll.

To make a rectangular parcel, place filling on crêpe and fold in the sides, then gently roll up. To make a cone, fold in half and half again to make a triangular shape. Open the top 'pocket' and carefully spoon in the filling.

To make a crêpe layer, place 1 crêpe on a serving plate and spread with some filling, then top with a second crêpe. Continue until all the crêpes and filling are used, ending with a crêpe if the stack is to be browned under the grill. Serve cut into wedges.

BASIC CRÊPES

125 g (4 oz/1 cup) plain flour
pinch of salt
2 eggs
315 ml (10 fl oz/1¼ cups) milk
3 teaspoons butter, melted
vegetable oil or lard for cooking
TO SERVE: lemon juice and sugar, or warmed jam

Sift flour and salt into a bowl. Make a well in centre and add eggs and a little milk. Beat, working in all flour. Beat in remaining milk and butter.

Heat a little vegetable oil or lard in a 17.5 cm (7 in) crêpe pan, barely covering the base. Pour in 2–3 tablespoons batter, tilting the pan so the batter covers the base thinly and evenly. Cook over high heat for about 1 minute, until lightly browned underneath.

Turn crêpe with a palette knife and cook other side for about 30 seconds. Remove from pan and keep warm, then continue until all the batter is used. Serve with lemon juice and sugar, with warmed jam or savoury or sweet toppings or fillings, see pages 20–55.

Makes 8.

WHOLEMEAL CRÊPES

125 g (4 oz/1 cup) plain wholemeal flour
½ teaspoon salt
3 eggs
315 ml (10 fl oz/1¼ cups) milk
vegetable oil or lard for cooking

Stir flour and salt into a bowl. Make a well in the centre and add the eggs and a little of the milk. Beat well with a wooden spoon, working in all the flour, then gradually beat in the remaining milk until the batter is bubbling.

Heat a little vegetable oil or lard in a 17.5 cm (7 in) crêpe pan, barely covering the base. Pour in 2–3 tablespoons batter, tilting the pan so the batter covers the base thinly and evenly. Cook over high heat for about 1 minute, until lightly browned underneath.

Turn crêpe with a palette knife and cook other side for about 30 seconds. Remove from pan and keep warm, then continue until all the batter is used. Serve with savoury or sweet toppings or fillings, see pages 20–55.

Makes 8.

BUCKWHEAT CRÊPES

60 g (2 oz/½ cup) buckwheat flour
60 g (2 oz/½ cup) plain flour
6 teaspoons wheatgerm
pinch of salt
2 eggs
6 teaspoons vegetable oil
315 ml (10 fl oz/1¼ cups) milk
vegetable oil or lard for cooking

In a bowl, stir together the flours, wheatgerm, and salt. In a jug, beat together the eggs and oil, then stir into the dry ingredients. Beat in enough milk to make a thick creamy batter.

Heat a little vegetable oil or lard in a 17.5 cm (7 in) crêpe pan, barely covering the base. Pour in enough batter to cover the base of pan thinly and evenly. Cook gently until surface is set and bubbling.

Turn crêpe with a palette knife and cook other side. Remove from pan and keep warm, then continue until all the batter is used. Serve the crêpes hot with any of the savoury or sweet toppings or fillings, see pages 20–55.

Makes 8.

OATMEAL CRÊPES

60 g (2 oz/½ cup) fine oatmeal
60 g (2 oz/½ cup) plain wholemeal flour
pinch of salt
2 eggs
3 teaspoons vegetable oil
315 ml (10 fl oz/1¼ cups) milk
vegetable oil or lard for cooking

In a bowl, stir together oatmeal, flour and salt. In a jug, beat together the eggs and oil, then stir into the dry ingredients. Beat in enough milk to make a thick creamy batter.

Heat a little vegetable oil or lard in a 17.5 cm (7 in) crêpe pan, barely covering the base. Pour in enough batter to cover the base of pan thinly and evenly. Cook gently until surface is set and bubbling.

Turn crêpe with a palette knife and cook other side. Remove from pan and keep warm, then continue until all the batter is used. Serve with savoury or sweet toppings or fillings, see pages 20–55.

Makes 8.

—— CORNMEAL PANCAKES ——

60 g (2 oz/½ cup) cornmeal
315 ml (10 fl oz/1¼ cups) boiling water
315 ml (10 fl oz/1¼ cups) milk
250 g (8 oz/2 cups) plain flour
30 g (1 oz/6 teaspoons) granulated sugar
2 teaspoons baking powder
1 teaspoon salt
1 egg, beaten
30 g (1 oz/6 teaspoons) butter, melted
vegetable oil or lard for cooking
TO SERVE: butter and maple syrup

Put the cornmeal into a small saucepan. Add the boiling water and simmer for 5 minutes, stirring well. Transfer to a bowl and beat in the milk. In a separate bowl, stir together flour, sugar, baking powder and salt, then beat into the cornmeal mixture. Beat in the egg and butter.

Heat a heavy-based frying pan and lightly grease with vegetable oil or lard. Pour in batter to make 7.5 cm (3 in) rounds and cook until surface of each pancake is just set and covered with tiny bubbles. Turn with a palette knife and continue cooking on other side until golden. Remove from pan and serve warm with butter and maple syrup.

Makes 24.

BLINI

375 g (12 oz/3 cups) buckwheat flour

625 ml (20 fl oz/2½ cups) milk

22 g (¾ oz/4½ teaspoons) fresh yeast or
3 teaspoons easy-blend dried yeast

3 eggs, separated

125 g (4 oz/½ cup) butter, softened

½ teaspoon salt

vegetable oil or lard for cooking

fresh mint sprig, to garnish

TO SERVE: caviar or lumpfish roe and
thick sour cream or yogurt

Put 125g (4 oz/1 cup) flour into a warm bowl. Heat 155 ml (5 fl oz/⅔ cup) milk in a saucepan until luke-warm. Blend the fresh yeast into the warm milk, then beat into the flour. Stir the easy-blend yeast into the flour, then mix in the warm milk. Cover and leave in a warm place for 1 hour, until risen and bubbling.

In a large bowl, beat egg yolks with butter, then gradually beat in the yeast mixture, remaining flour and milk and the salt. Beat well until smooth. Cover and leave in a warm place for 30 minutes, to rise.

In a separate bowl, whisk egg whites to stiff peaks and fold into the batter. Heat a heavy-based frying pan and lightly grease with vegetable oil or lard. Pour in batter to make 7.5 cm (3 in) rounds and cook until surface of each blini is just set and covered with bubbles. Turn with a palette knife and continue cooking on other side until golden. Remove from the pan and serve with caviar or lump fish roe and thick sour cream, or yogurt, or any smoked or salted fish. Garnish with a sprig of fresh mint.

Makes 15–18.

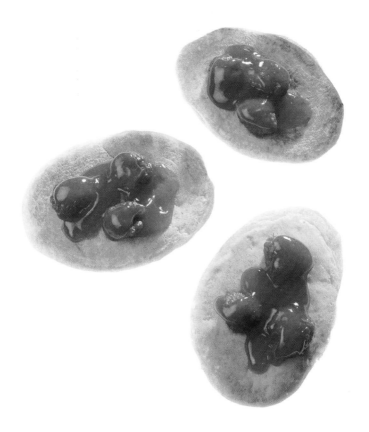

PUFFY YEAST PANCAKES

250 g (8 oz/2 cups) plain flour

1 teaspoon sugar

15 g (½ oz/ 3 teaspoons) fresh yeast or
2 teaspoons easy-blend dried yeast

315 ml (10 fl oz/1¼ cups) milk

1 egg, separated

½ teaspoon salt

vegetable oil or lard for cooking

Sift flour into a bowl, then stir in the sugar and blend or stir in the yeast. Heat milk in a saucepan until lukewarm and beat into the flour until smooth. Cover and leave in a warm place for 30 minutes, until risen and bubbling, stirring occasionally with a wooden spoon.

Stir egg yolk into risen batter. In a separate bowl, whisk egg white to stiff peaks and stir in salt, then fold into the batter.

Lightly grease a heavy-based frying pan with vegetable oil or lard. Fry single tablespoons of the batter over medium heat, turning each pancake when golden on base and continue cooking on other side until set and lightly browned. Lift cooked pancakes onto a sheet of sugared greaseproof paper. Serve at once with sweet toppings, see pages 28–37.

Makes 15.

POTATO PANCAKES

2 large potatoes, peeled, if desired
60 g (2 oz/½ cup) plain flour
2 eggs
185 ml (6 fl oz/¾ cup) milk
salt and pepper
vegetable oil or lard for cooking

Boil potatoes in salted water for 10 minutes, until part-cooked. Drain well and coarsely grate into a bowl, then stir in the flour. Beat eggs and milk together until well mixed, then gradually work into potatoes, beating with a wooden spoon. Season well with salt and pepper.

Lightly grease a heavy-based frying pan with vegetable oil or lard. Heat pan, pour in about 4 tablespoons of potato mixture to make 0.5 cm (¼ in) layer, and cook until golden on base, then turn and cook on the other side. Remove from pan and keep warm, then continue until all the batter is used. Serve hot with savoury toppings, see pages 20–27.

Makes 4–6.

SEAFOOD TOPPING

30 g (1 oz/6 teaspoons) butter

1 small red pepper (capsicum), seeded and finely chopped

30 g (1 oz/¼ cup) plain flour

315 ml (10 fl oz/1¼ cups) milk

60 g (2 oz/½ cup) finely grated Cheddar cheese

250 g (8 oz) smoked haddock fillets, cooked, skinned and flaked

125 g (4 oz) peeled cooked prawns, thawed if frozen

½ teaspoon dry mustard

lemon slices and fresh parsley sprigs, to garnish

Melt butter in a saucepan, add pepper (capsicum) and cook over low heat until pepper (capsicum) is just soft. Add flour and cook for 1 minute, stirring, then remove from heat and gradually stir in milk. Return to heat and bring to boil, stirring until sauce is thickened.

Stir in cheese, haddock, prawns and mustard over low heat until warm. Serve hot with any crêpes, garnished with lemon and parsley.

Serves 4.

— EGG & TOMATO TOPPING —

15 g (½ oz/3 teaspoons) butter
1 onion, chopped
440 g (14 oz) can tomatoes
salt and pepper
½ teaspoon sugar
3 teaspoons Worcestershire sauce
6 hard-boiled eggs, chopped
fresh watercress sprigs, to garnish

Melt butter in a saucepan, add onion and cook over low heat for 5 minutes, until soft. Add tomatoes and their juice, salt and pepper, sugar and Worcestershire sauce and simmer, uncovered, for 10 minutes, until slightly thickened.

Stir eggs into the tomato mixture and simmer for 2 minutes, stirring well. Serve hot with any crêpes, garnished with watercress.

Serves 4.

MEXICAN TOPPING

250 g (8 oz) lean minced beef
1 stick celery, finely chopped
1 onion, finely chopped
440 g (14 oz) can tomatoes
220 g (7 oz) can sweetcorn kernels, well drained
6 teaspoons tomato purée (paste)
2 teaspoons chilli powder
celery leaves, to garnish

Put beef, celery and onion into a saucepan and cook gently, over medium heat, stirring well, for 5 minutes. Drain off surplus fat.

Stir in tomatoes with their juice, sweetcorn kernels, tomato purée (paste) and chilli powder. Simmer over low heat, uncovered, stirring occasionally, for 10 minutes, until slightly reduced. Serve hot with any crêpes, garnished with celery leaves.

Serves 4.

─── HAM & CHEESE TOPPING ───

30 g (1 oz/6 teaspoons) butter

100 g (4 oz) mushrooms, thinly sliced

250 g (8 oz) lean cooked ham, finely chopped

fresh watercress sprigs, to garnish

CHEESE SAUCE:

30 g (1 oz/6 teaspoons) butter

30 g (1 oz/¼ cup) plain flour

315 ml (10 fl oz/1¼ cups) milk

125 g (4 oz/1 cup) grated Cheddar cheese

salt and pepper

To make cheese sauce, melt butter in a saucepan over low heat, then stir in flour and cook for 1 minute. Remove from heat and gradually stir in milk. Return to heat and bring to the boil, stirring until thickened. Remove from heat and stir in cheese, stirring until cheese melts. Season with salt and pepper. Set aside.

Melt butter in a saucepan over low heat, add mushrooms and stir for 3 minutes. Stir in ham and cook for 1 minute. Gently reheat cheese sauce and stir in mushroom and ham mixture. Serve hot with any crêpes, garnished with watercress.

Serves 4.

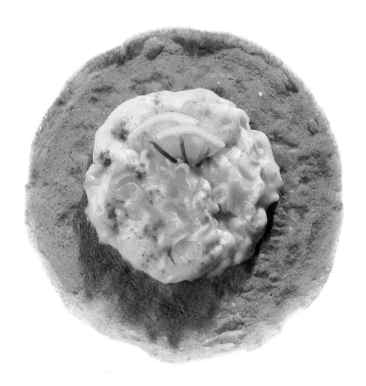

— SALMON & LEMON TOPPING —

125 g (4 oz) smoked salmon, cut into
thin strips

cayenne pepper

lemon slices and chopped fresh chives,
to garnish

LEMON SAUCE:

30 g (1 oz/6 teaspoons) butter

30 g (1 oz/¼ cup) plain flour

315 ml (10 fl oz/1¼ cups) milk

9 teaspoons lemon juice

2 egg yolks, beaten

salt and pepper

To make the lemon sauce, melt
butter in a saucepan over low heat,
then stir in flour and cook for 1
minute. Remove from heat and
gradually stir in milk. Return to the
heat and bring to the boil, stirring
until thickened. Stir in lemon juice,
then remove from heat and stir in
yolks. Season to taste with salt and
pepper.

Lightly sprinkle the smoked
salmon with cayenne pepper and
stir into the sauce. Serve topping
warm, garnished with lemon slices
and chopped chives.

Serves 4.

FARMHOUSE TOPPING

125 g (4 oz) lean bacon, rind removed and diced

30 g (1 oz/6 teaspoons) butter

250 g (8 oz) button mushrooms, thinly sliced

125 g (4 oz) cold cooked chicken, diced

155 ml (5 fl oz/⅔ cup) single (light) cream

salt and pepper

fresh mint leaves, to garnish

Put bacon into a saucepan and cook gently over low heat for 5 minutes, until cooked and the fat has run out. Add the butter and mushrooms and continue cooking over low heat for 5 minutes, stirring often. Stir in the chicken and heat through.

Remove from heat and stir in the cream until the bacon, mushrooms and chicken are coated. Return to the heat and very gently warm through. Do not boil or the cream may curdle. Season with salt and pepper to taste. Serve as a topping or filling, garnished with fresh mint leaves.

Serves 4.

– SAUSAGE & BACON TOPPING –

4 thin pork sausages

4 lean rashers bacon, rinds removed and coarsely chopped

125 g (4 oz) button mushrooms, thinly sliced

1 teaspoon chopped fresh chives, plus extra to garnish

Grill sausages until golden brown, then cut each into 8 thick slices and set aside.

Put bacon into a pan and heat gently until crisp and all the fat has run out. Stir in mushrooms and cook over low heat for 3 minutes, then stir in sausages and chives and heat through. Serve as a topping or filling, garnished with extra chopped and whole chives.

Serves 4.

— BACON PINEAPPLE TOPPING —

250 g (8 oz) bacon rashers, rinds removed
and coarsely chopped

8 canned pineapple rings in natural
juice, drained and cut into eighths

fresh watercress sprigs, to garnish

Put bacon into a saucepan and heat
gently until crisp and all the fat has
run out.

Stir pineapple into pan and heat
through. Serve as a topping or filling,
garnished with watercress.

Serves 4.

Note: 6 teaspoons of drained pineapple juice can be used to replace
the rum in Jamaican Banana Topping, see page 37, if preparing for
children.

– HONEYED BANANA TOPPING –

3 bananas
2 teaspoons lemon juice
4 tablespoons clear honey
pinch of grated nutmeg

Peel the bananas and slice into strips. Put them into a bowl, add lemon juice and toss well so the slices are coated, to prevent browning.

Put honey into a small saucepan and warm over low heat. Add bananas and heat through until just warm, then season with nutmeg. Serve with any crêpes.

Serves 4.

RASPBERRY TOPPING

375 g (12 oz) frozen raspberries, thawed
30 g (1 oz/6 teaspoons) sugar
3 teaspoons cornflour
raspberry leaves, to decorate, if desired

Drain raspberries and put juice into a small saucepan with 155 ml (5 fl oz/ ⅔ cup) water and sugar and bring to the boil. Mix cornflour with 6 teaspoons cold water in a bowl, then add the boiling liquid, stirring well. Return to pan and bring to the boil over low heat until mixture thickens, stirring constantly.

Remove from heat and stir in raspberries. Return to heat and heat gently without breaking up fruit. Serve with any crêpes, decorated with raspberry leaves, if desired.

Serves 4.

— HONEY & ORANGE TOPPING —

2 oranges
9 teaspoons lemon juice
4 tablespoons clear honey
toasted coconut and orange peel strips, to decorate

Peel the oranges, carefully removing all white pith. Using a sharp knife, cut between the membranes and remove the orange segments, reserving the juice.

Put reserved orange juice, lemon juice and honey into a saucepan and heat gently for 3 minutes. Add orange segments and stir over low heat for 2 minutes. Serve with any crêpes, decorated with toasted coconut and orange peel strips.

Serves 4.

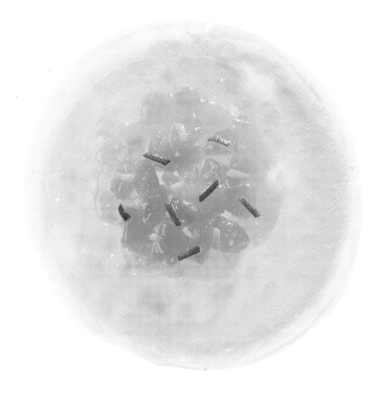

– APRICOT & LEMON TOPPING –

60 g (2 oz/½ cup) dried apricots, chopped and soaked overnight
5 tablespoons apricot jam
1 teaspoon grated lemon or lime peel
6 teaspoons lemon juice
slivers of lemon or lime peel, to decorate

Drain the apricots and put into a saucepan with 90 ml (3 fl oz/generous ⅓ cup) of the soaking liquid, then simmer over low heat for 5 minutes.

Add apricot jam and lemon or lime peel and juice and stir over low heat for 5 minutes, until well blended. Serve with any crêpes, decorated with slivers of lemon or lime peel.

Serves 4.

Note: Many large supermarkets and health food shops stock presoaked dried apricots, which eliminates the need for overnight soaking.

— BANANA CREAM TOPPING —

155 ml (5 fl oz/⅔ cup) whipping cream
2 large bananas
30 g (1 oz/2 tablespoons) icing sugar
2 teaspoons lemon juice
½ teaspoon grated nutmeg
pecan nuts and extra nutmeg, to decorate, if desired

In a bowl, whip the cream to soft peaks. Mash the bananas in a separate bowl with the sugar and lemon juice.

Fold the cream into the banana mixture and add the nutmeg. Put into a serving bowl. Cover and chill until ready to serve. If desired, serve decorated with pecan nuts and extra nutmeg.

Serves 4.

— BUTTERSCOTCH TOPPING —

125 g (4 oz/¾ cup) dark moist brown sugar
30 g (1 oz/¼ cup) plain. flour
125 g (4 oz/½ cup) butter, softened
125 ml (4 fl oz/½ cup) milk
toasted almonds, to decorate

Put sugar, flour and butter into a bowl and beat with a wooden spoon until well mixed. Transfer to a saucepan and heat gently until butter melts and mixture bubbles, then stir over low heat for 3 minutes.

Remove from heat and gradually add milk. Return to heat and beat until smooth and the mixture is boiling. Put into a warm serving bowl. To serve, decorate with toasted almonds.

Serves 4.

— ORANGE LIQUEUR TOPPING —

60 g (2 oz/¼ cup) butter, softened
125 g (4 oz/¾ cup) icing sugar
finely grated peel and juice of 1 orange
6 teaspoons orange-flavoured liqueur
orange segments and lemon peel strips,
to decorate

Cream the butter and icing sugar in a bowl until light and fluffy.

Gradually beat orange peel and juice into the butter mixture, then gradually add the orange liqueur, beating until soft and creamy. Turn into a serving bowl and chill for at least 30 minutes before serving. To serve, pipe or spoon onto a flat crêpe. Decorate with orange segments and lemon peel strips.

Serves 4.

Note: For children, the orange-flavoured liqueur can be replaced with additional orange juice.

– APPLE & SULTANA TOPPING –

500 g (1 lb) cooking apples, peeled, cored and thinly sliced
90 g (3 oz/⅓ cup) sugar
60 g (2 oz/⅓ cup) sultanas
2 teaspoons lemon juice
¼ teaspoon ground cinnamon
apple peel leaves, to decorate

Put the apple slices into a saucepan with 155 ml (5 fl oz/⅔ cup) water and the sugar and cook over low heat until the apples are soft. Press through a sieve or purée in a blender or food processor.

Return apple purée to pan and simmer for 5 minutes, until thick. Stir in the sultanas, lemon juice and cinnamon and simmer for 1 minute. Turn into a warm serving bowl. To serve, decorate with leaves cut from a piece of apple peel.

Serves 4.

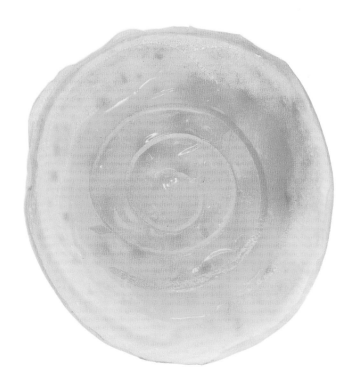

── FRESH LEMON TOPPING ──

finely grated peel and juice of 2 lemons
60 g (2 oz/¼ cup) sugar
6 teaspoons cornflour
6 teaspoons lemon curd
lemon peel strips, to decorate

Put lemon peel and juice into a saucepan with 250 ml (8 fl oz/1 cup) water and the sugar. Heat gently until the sugar has dissolved.

Mix the cornflour with 60 ml (2 fl oz/¼ cup) water in a bowl. Add a little of the hot liquid and stir well, then return to the pan with the lemon curd. Stir over low heat until the sauce is thick and glossy. Turn into a warm serving bowl. To serve, decorate with lemon peel strips.

Serves 4.

- JAMAICAN BANANA TOPPING -

125 g (4 oz/½ cup) butter

125 g (4 oz/¾ cup) dark moist brown sugar

finely grated peel and juice of 1 lemon

3 medium bananas

6 teaspoons dark rum

lemon twists and lemon peel strips, to decorate

Put butter and sugar into a saucepan and stir over low heat until the butter has melted. Stir the lemon peel and juice into the butter and continue simmering for 1 minute.

Peel the bananas and slice thinly. Stir into the sugar mixture. Warm through for 2 minutes, then remove from heat and stir in rum. Turn into a warm serving bowl. To serve, decorate with lemon twists and lemon peel strips.

Serves 4.

— CHEESY ANCHOVY CRÊPES —

eight 17.5 cm (7 in) crêpes, see pages 12-15

90 g (3 oz) can anchovies, drained

125 g (4 oz) Gruyère cheese, cut into thin strips, plus extra, grated, to garnish

155 ml (5 fl oz/⅔ cup) thick sour cream

1 tablespoon lemon juice

salt and pepper

1 tablespoon chopped fresh parsley

Keep crêpes warm while preparing filling. Reserve 4 anchovy fillets for garnish, and finely chop the remainder. Mix together cheese, anchovies, thick sour cream and lemon juice, then season with salt and pepper, remembering the anchovies are very salty.

Divide filling between crêpes and roll up. Place on a serving dish and sprinkle with chopped parsley. Garnish with reserved anchovy fillets and extra grated cheese and serve at once.

Serves 4.

MOZZARELLA CRÊPES

eight 17.5 cm (7 in) crêpes, see pages
12-15

60 g (2 oz/¼ cup) butter

2.5 cm (1 in) thick slice bread, cubed

100 g (4 oz) diced Mozzarella cheese

salt and pepper

30 g (1 oz/¼ cup) grated Parmesan
cheese

fresh basil sprigs, to garnish

Keep crêpes warm while preparing filling. Heat butter in a frying pan and fry the bread cubes until golden on all sides. Remove from heat, stir in cheese and season to taste with salt and pepper.

Divide filling between crêpes and roll up. Put in a single layer in a shallow flameproof serving dish, sprinkle with Parmesan cheese and brown under a hot grill for 2 minutes, until the Parmesan is light golden and bubbling. Garnish with basil sprigs and serve.

Serves 4.

ITALIAN RICOTTA CRÊPES

eight 17.5 cm (7 in) crêpes, see pages 12–15

250 g (8 oz/1 cup) ricotta cheese

3 teaspoons grated Parmesan cheese

3 teaspoons chopped fresh majoram or 1½ teaspoons dried

salt and pepper

30 g (1 oz/6 teaspoons) butter

2 teaspoons plain flour

6 teaspoons tomato purée (paste)

155 ml (5 fl oz/⅔ cup) chicken stock

fresh marjoram sprigs, to garnish

Keep crêpes warm while preparing filling. Put ricotta cheese into a bowl with Parmesan cheese, marjoram and salt and pepper, then beat until creamy and well blended.

Divide filling between crêpes and fold into quarters. Put in a single layer in a shallow flameproof serving dish.

Melt butter in a small saucepan over medium heat and stir in flour. Cook for 30 seconds, stirring, then work in tomato purée (paste) and stock, stirring. Season to taste with salt and pepper and continue simmering for 3 minutes, stirring occasionally.

Spoon over crêpes and put under a hot grill for 2 minutes, until bubbling. Garnish with fresh marjoram sprigs and serve at once.

Serves 4.

PARMESAN CRÊPES

eight 17.5 cm (7 in) crêpes, see pages 12-15

2 tablespoons vegetable oil

30 g (1 oz/6 teaspoons) butter

250 g (8 oz) potatoes, cooked and diced

salt and pepper

60 g (2 oz/1 cup) fresh breadcrumbs

60 g (2 oz/¼ cup) butter, melted

3 teaspoons chopped fresh parsley

60 g (2 oz/½ cup) grated Parmesan cheese

fresh parsley sprigs, to garnish

Keep crêpes warm while preparing filling. Heat oil and butter in a frying pan and cook potatoes until crisp and golden. Drain well on absorbent kitchen paper, then season to taste with salt and pepper.

Divide potato cubes between crêpes and fold into quarters. Put in a single layer in a shallow flameproof serving dish. Mix together breadcrumbs, melted butter and chopped parsley, then sprinkle over crêpes with Parmesan cheese. Put under a medium grill for 4–5 minutes, until crisp and golden. Garnish with fresh parsley sprigs and serve at once.

Serves 4.

ASPARAGUS CRÊPES

eight 17.5 cm (7 in) crêpes, see pages 12-15

375 g (12 oz) fresh or canned asparagus tips

30 g (1 oz/6 teaspoons) butter

2 teaspoons plain flour

155 ml (5 fl oz/⅔ cup) single (light) cream

1 teaspoon chopped fresh parsley

1 teaspoon chopped fresh chives

salt and pepper

1 tablespoon grated Parmesan cheese

Keep crêpes warm while preparing filling. If asparagus is fresh, cook in boiling salted water for 6 minutes, then drain well. If canned, drain well.

Melt butter into a saucepan over low heat, then stir in flour and cook for 30 seconds. Stir in cream and continue cooking gently until thick, then stir in parsley and chives and season to taste with salt and pepper.

Stir asparagus tips into sauce. Divide filling between crêpes and roll up. Put in a single layer in a shallow flameproof serving dish, sprinkle with Parmesan cheese and brown under a hot grill for 2 minutes, until the Parmesan is light golden and bubbling.

Serves 4.

Note: Garnish with extra asparagus tips, if desired.

SWEETCORN LAYERS

eight 17.5 cm (7 in) crêpes, see pages 12-15

1 onion, finely chopped

30 g (1 oz/6 teaspoons) butter

440 g (14 oz) can sweetcorn kernels, drained

1 quantity Cheese Sauce, see page 23

1 teaspoon chopped fresh marjoram

30 g (1 oz/¼ cup) grated Cheddar cheese

fresh marjoram sprigs, to garnish

Keep crêpes warm while preparing filling. Put onion and butter into a saucepan and cook over low heat for 5 minutes, until soft, then stir in sweetcorn kernels and heat through.

Reserve 6 tablespoons cheese sauce and mix the remainder with the corn, then add the marjoram.

Put one crêpe on a large flame-proof serving plate and spread with some of the corn mixture. Top with a second crêpe and repeat until all the crêpes and corn mixture are used, finishing with a crêpe.

Spread reserved cheese sauce on top and sprinkle with grated cheese. Brown under a hot grill for 3 minutes, until sauce is bubbling. Garnish with fresh marjoram and serve at once, cut into wedges.

Serves 4.

NEAPOLITAN CRÊPES

eight 17.5 cm (7 in) crêpes, see pages 12-15

30 g (1 oz/6 teaspoons) butter

3 teaspoons olive oil

500 g (1 lb) onions, thinly sliced

440 g (14 oz) can tomatoes

90 g (3 oz) can anchovies, drained and chopped

3 tablespoons tomato purée (paste)

8 stuffed olives, sliced

1 teaspoon chopped fresh basil

salt and pepper, to taste

fresh basil sprigs and extra stuffed olives, to garnish

Keep crêpes warm while preparing filling. Heat butter and oil in a saucepan, add onions and cook over low heat for 5 minutes, until soft. Add tomatoes and their juice, anchovies, tomato purée (paste), olives, basil and salt and pepper, then cover and simmer for 20 minutes, stirring occasionally.

Preheat oven to 180C (350F/Gas 4). Divide filling between crêpes and roll up. Put in a single layer in a shallow ovenproof serving dish, cover with foil and heat through in the oven for 20 minutes. Garnish with basil sprigs and sliced olives and serve hot.

Serves 4.

——— MUSHROOM CRÊPES ———

eight 17.5 cm (7 in) crêpes, see pages 12-15

60 g (2 oz/¼ cup) butter

250 g (8 oz) mushrooms, thinly sliced

60 g (2 oz/½ cup) plain flour

315 ml (10 fl oz/1¼ cups) milk

¼ teaspoon grated nutmeg

salt and pepper

chopped fresh parsley and sprigs and mushroom slices, to garnish

Keep crêpes warm while preparing filling. Melt butter in a large saucepan, add mushrooms, cover and cook over low heat for 5 minutes.

Stir in the flour and cook for 1 minute, stirring, then gradually add milk, stirring well. Bring to the boil and simmer for 3 minutes. Season with nutmeg and salt and pepper.

Preheat oven to 180C (350F/Gas 4). Divide filling between crêpes. Roll up and put in a single layer in a shallow ovenproof serving dish, cover with foil and heat through in the oven for 20 minutes. Garnish with chopped parsley and sprigs and mushroom slices. Serve hot.

Serves 4.

SPINACH CRÊPES

eight 17.5 cm (7 in) crêpes, see pages 12-15

1 kg (2 lb) fresh spinach, stalks removed

1 onion, finely chopped

30 g (1 oz/6 teaspoons) butter

3 teaspoons tomato purée (paste)

1 teaspoon paprika

salt and pepper

2 hard-boiled eggs, chopped

30 g (1 oz/¼ cup) grated Parmesan cheese

fresh parsley sprigs, to garnish

Keep crêpes warm while preparing filling. Wash spinach very well and put into a large saucepan with only the water clinging to its leaves. Cover and heat gently until spinach is cooked and very tender. Drain well and press out excess moisture, then finely chop and set aside.

Put onion and butter into a large pan and cook over low heat for 5 minutes, until soft. Stir in tomato purée (paste) and paprika and simmer for 2 minutes. Season with salt and pepper and stir in eggs.

Divide spinach between crêpes and spread over surface, then top with egg mixture and roll up. Put in a single layer in a shallow flameproof serving dish, sprinkle with Parmesan cheese and brown under a hot grill for 2 minutes, until the Parmesan is light golden and bubbling. Garnish with parsley sprigs and serve.

Serves 4.

SMOKED TROUT CRÊPES

eight 17.5 cm/7 in crêpes, see pages 12-15

185 g (6 oz) smoked trout, skinned, boned and flaked

3 spring onions, finely chopped

125 g (4 oz/½ cup) cream cheese

2 tablespoons single (light) cream

1 teaspoon lemon juice

salt and pepper

spring onion flower, to garnish

Keep crêpes warm while preparing filling. Put trout, onions, cream cheese and cream into a bowl and beat together until soft and well mixed. Add lemon juice and season with salt and pepper.

Preheat oven to 150C (300F/Gas 2). Divide mixture between crêpes and roll up. Put in a single layer in a shallow ovenproof serving dish and warm through in the oven for 15 minutes. Garnish with a spring onion flower and serve hot.

Serves 4.

Note: To make a spring onion flower, cut off a 7.5 cm (3 in) piece of stalk and finely shred, leaving the bottom 2.5 cm (1 in) whole. Soak in iced water for 1 hour.

— SALMON SUPREME CRÊPES —

eight 17.5 cm (7 in) crêpes, see pages 12-15

1 onion, finely chopped

60 g (2 oz) button mushrooms, thinly sliced

30 g (1 oz/6 teaspoons) butter

30 g (1 oz/¼ cup) plain flour

155 ml (5 fl oz/⅔ cup) single (light) cream

220 g (7 oz) can red salmon, well drained and flaked

125 g (4 oz) cooked peas

60 g (2 oz/½ cup) grated Gruyère cheese

1 teaspoon lemon juice

salt and pepper

30 g (1 oz/¼ cup) grated Parmesan cheese

fresh parsley sprig and lemon twist, to garnish

Keep crêpes warm while preparing filling. Put onion, mushrooms and butter into a saucepan and cook over low heat for 5 minutes, until onion is soft. Stir in flour and cook for 1 minute, stirring, then remove from heat and stir in cream. Cook over low heat, stirring until thick and smooth, without boiling. Remove from heat and stir in salmon, peas, Gruyère cheese, lemon juice and salt and pepper.

Preheat oven to 180C (350F/Gas 4). Divide filling between crêpes and roll up. Put in a single layer in a shallow ovenproof serving dish, sprinkle with Parmesan cheese and warm through in the oven for 25 minutes. Garnish with fresh parsley sprig and lemon twist and serve at once.

Serves 4.

FISH CRESPOLINI

eight 17.5 cm (7 in) crêpes, see pages 12-15

375 g (12 oz) white fish fillets, such as cod

470 ml (15 fl oz/2 cups) milk

30 g (1 oz/6 teaspoons) butter

30 g (1 oz/¼ cup) plain flour

4 tomatoes, skinned, seeded and chopped

3 teaspoons lemon juice

salt and pepper

90 g (3 oz/¾ cup) grated Cheddar cheese

watercress sprigs and sliced cherry tomatoes, to garnish

Keep crêpes warm while preparing filling. Put fish into a saucepan with half the milk and poach until fish is cooked through but unbroken. Drain and reserve cooking liquid. Skin and flake fish and set aside.

Melt butter in a saucepan over low heat, stir in flour and cook for 30 seconds. Remove from heat and stir in reserved liquid and remaining milk. Return to low heat and cook gently, stirring, until thick and smooth. Divide sauce in half.

Preheat oven to 190C (375F/Gas 5). Stir fish, tomatoes and lemon juice into half of the sauce and season with salt and pepper. Divide fish mixture between crêpes and roll up. Put in a single layer in a shallow ovenproof serving dish. Stir cheese into remaining sauce and spoon over crêpes. Heat through in the oven for 20 minutes, until sauce is bubbling. Garnish with watercress sprigs and sliced cherry tomatoes.

Serves 4.

—— PRAWN & TUNA CRÊPES ——

eight 17.5 cm (7 in) crêpes, see pages 12-15

45 g (1½ oz/9 teaspoons) butter

1 small green pepper (capsicum), cored, seeded and finely chopped

15 g (½ oz/6 teaspoons) plain flour

155 ml (5 fl oz/⅔ cup) chicken stock

125 g (4 oz) peeled cooked prawns, thawed if frozen

220 g (7 oz) can tuna in brine, drained and flaked

155 ml (5 fl oz/⅔ cup) single (light) cream

salt and pepper

peeled prawns, fresh tarragon sprigs and lemon slices, to garnish

Keep crêpes warm while preparing filling. Melt butter in a saucepan, add green pepper (capsicum) and cook over low heat until just soft. Add flour and cook for 1 minute, stirring well.

Stir in chicken stock and simmer over low heat, stirring, until thick. Stir in prawns. Add tuna to pan, stir in cream and heat through but do not boil. Season to taste with salt and pepper.

Preheat oven to 180C (350F/Gas 4). Divide mixture between crêpes. Roll up and put in a single layer in a shallow ovenproof serving dish. Cover with foil and heat in the oven for 15 minutes. Garnish with peeled prawns, tarragon sprigs and lemon slices and serve hot.

Serves 4.

— HADDOCK & EGG CRÊPES —

eight 17.5 cm (7 in) crêpes, see pages
12-15

250 g (8 oz) smoked haddock fillets

315 ml (10 fl oz/1¼ cups) milk

30 g (1 oz/6 teaspoons) butter

30 g (1 oz/¼ cup) plain flour

3 teaspoons lemon juice

2 hard-boiled eggs, chopped

2 teaspoons chopped fresh dill

30 g (1 oz/¼ cup) grated Parmesan
cheese

fresh dill sprigs and lemon slices,
to garnish

Keep crêpes warm while preparing
filling. Put haddock into a saucepan
with milk and poach until fish is
cooked through but unbroken.
Drain milk and reserve. Skin and
flake fish and set aside.

Melt butter in a pan over low
heat, stir in flour and cook for 30
seconds. Remove from heat and stir
in reserved cooking milk. Return
to low heat and cook gently, stirring, until the sauce is thick and
smooth.

Remove from heat and stir in
haddock, lemon juice, eggs and
dill. Divide mixture between crêpes.
Roll up and arrange in a single layer
in a shallow flameproof serving dish,
sprinkle with Parmesan cheese and
brown under a hot grill for 2
minutes, until the Parmesan is light
golden and bubbling. Garnish each
portion with fresh dill sprigs and
lemon slices.

Serves 4.

BEEF CRÊPES

eight 17.5 cm (7 in) crêpes, see pages 12-15

1 quantity Cheese Sauce, see page 23

1 onion, finely chopped

15 g (½ oz/3 teaspoons) butter

375 g (12 oz) lean minced beef

155 ml (5 fl oz/⅔ cup) beef stock

2 tablespoons tomato purée (paste)

pinch of dried thyme

salt and pepper

3 teaspoons finely grated Parmesan cheese

chopped fresh chives, to garnish

Prepare the crêpes and cheese sauce and keep warm while preparing meat filling. Put onion and butter into a pan and cook over low heat for 5 minutes, until onion is soft. Stir in meat and cook over low heat for 5 minutes, then add stock, tomato purée (paste), thyme and salt and pepper. Cover and simmer for 15 minutes.

Divide meat mixture between crêpes. Place the crêpes close together in a single layer in a flame-proof serving dish, spoon over the cheese sauce, sprinkle with Parmesan cheese and put under a hot grill for 2-3 minutes, until golden brown and bubbling. Garnish with chopped chives.

Serves 4.

── CURRIED CHICKEN CRÊPES ──

eight 17.5 cm (7 in) crêpes, see pages 12-15

1 onion, finely chopped

30 g (1 oz/6 teaspoons) butter

2 teaspoons curry powder

30 g (1 oz/¼ cup) plain flour

315 ml (10 fl oz/1¼ cups) chicken stock

375 g (12 oz) cold cooked chicken, diced

3 teaspoons lemon juice

salt and pepper

slices of green pepper (capsicum), lemon and fresh mint sprigs, to garnish

Keep crêpes warm while preparing filling. Put onion and butter into a saucepan and cook over low heat for 5 minutes, until soft. Stir in curry powder and cook for 30 seconds, then stir in flour and cook for 30 seconds. Gradually add stock and bring to the boil, stirring constantly.

Stir in chicken and lemon juice and season with salt and pepper. Stir over low heat for 10 minutes. Divide chicken mixture between crêpes, roll up, garnish with slices of green pepper (capsicum), lemon and mint sprigs and serve at once.

Serves 4.

BOLOGNESE CRÊPES

eight 17.5 cm (7 in) crêpes, see pages 12-15

1 small clove garlic, crushed

1 large onion, finely chopped

30 g (1 oz/6 teaspoons) butter

500 g (1 lb) lean minced beef

30 g (1 oz/¼ cup) plain flour

440 g (14 oz) can tomatoes

2 teaspoons tomato purée (paste)

salt and pepper

30 g (1 oz/¼ cup) grated Parmesan cheese

watercress sprigs and tomato halves, to garnish

Keep crêpes warm while preparing filling. Put garlic and onion into a saucepan with butter and cook over low heat for 5 minutes, until onion is soft.

Add meat and cook over low heat for 5 minutes, stirring to break up meat. Stir in flour and cook for 1 minute, then add tomatoes with juice and tomato purée (paste). Stir well and simmer, uncovered, for 10 minutes, until thickened. Season to taste with salt and pepper.

Put one crêpe on a flameproof serving plate and spread with some filling. Top with a second crêpe and repeat until all the crêpes and filling are used, finishing with a crêpe. Sprinkle with Parmesan cheese, and brown under a hot grill for 2 minutes. Serve at once, cut into wedges. Garnish each portion with watercress sprigs and tomato halves.

Serves 4.

—— SWEET & SOUR CRÊPES ——

eight 17.5 cm (7 in) crêpes, see pages 12-15
250 g (8 oz) boneless shoulder pork, cubed
15 g (½ oz/3 teaspoons) lard
220 g (7 oz) can pineapple pieces in syrup
3 teaspoons redcurrant jelly
3 teaspoons moist brown sugar
3 teaspoons white wine vinegar
3 teaspoons cornflour
155 ml (5 fl oz/⅔ cup) tomato juice
salt and pepper
fresh watercress sprigs or bean sprouts and spring onion tassels, to garnish

Keep crêpes warm while preparing filling. Put pork and lard into a saucepan and fry over low heat for 10 minutes, until meat is tender and cooked through.

Drain pineapple, and put syrup into a pan with redcurrant jelly, sugar, vinegar, cornflour and tomato juice, then bring to the boil, stirring constantly. Simmer, uncovered, until thick, then stir in pork and pineapple pieces and season to taste with salt and pepper.

Preheat oven to 190C (375F/Gas 5). Divide pork mixture between crêpes. Roll up and put in a single layer in a shallow ovenproof serving dish. Cover crêpes with foil and heat through in the oven for 20 minutes. Garnish with watercress sprigs or bean sprouts and spring onion tassels and serve hot, straight from the dish.

Serves 4.

CARIBBEAN CRÊPES

eight 17.5 cm (7 in) crêpes, see pages
12-15

4 bananas

2 teaspoons lemon juice

155 ml (5 fl oz/⅔ cup) whipping cream

30 g (1 oz/2 tablespoons) dark moist
brown sugar

½ teaspoon grated nutmeg

Keep crêpes warm while preparing filling. Peel bananas and thinly slice one, then sprinkle with lemon juice and set aside. Whip cream to stiff peaks, and set aside about one-quarter for decoration.

Mash the remaining bananas and fold into cream with sugar and nutmeg. Divide mixture between crêpes and roll up firmly. Place on a serving dish and decorate with piped rosettes of cream and banana slices sprinkled with nutmeg.

Serves 4.

Variation: To make crêpes into mini cornets, cut each in half and roll into cornets. Carefully spoon the filling into the pockets, then decorate.

— APRICOT MERINGUE CRÊPES —

eight 17.5 cm (7 in) crêpes, see pages
12-15

90 g (3 oz/¼ cup) apricot jam

3 teaspoons lemon juice

2 egg whites

125 g (4 oz/½ cup) caster sugar

8 glacé cherries, halved

angelica 'leaves', to decorate

Keep the crêpes warm while preparing the filling. Put the jam and lemon juice into a saucepan and heat gently, stirring, until well mixed. Put one crêpe on a large ovenproof serving plate and spread with a thin layer of warm jam. Cover with second crêpe, and repeat until all the crêpes and apricot jam are used, finishing with a crêpe.

Preheat oven to 230C (450F/Gas 8). In a bowl, whisk egg whites to stiff peaks, then fold in the sugar. Lightly spread meringue on top crêpe and arrange cherries on top. Bake for 2 minutes, until pale golden. Decorate with angelica 'leaves', then serve at once, cut into wedges.

Serves 4.

— CHERRY & ALMOND LAYER —

eight 17.5 cm (7 in) crêpes, see pages
12-15

440 g (14 oz) can cherries

90 g (3 oz/¼ cup) cherry jam

3 teaspoons lemon juice

60 g (2 oz/½ cup) ground almonds

2 ripe eating pears, peeled and
thinly sliced

3 teaspoons icing sugar

Keep crêpes warm while preparing filling. Drain cherries, reserving juice. Put jam into a small saucepan and warm over low heat until just runny, then stir in 6 teaspoons cherry juice and the lemon juice, almonds and pears. Remove from heat and stir in cherries.

Preheat oven to 160C (325F/Gas 3). Put one crêpe on a large oven-proof serving plate. Spread with some filling and top with a second crêpe. Repeat until all the crêpes and cherry mixture are used, finishing with a crêpe on the top. Heat through in the oven for 10 minutes, then sift icing sugar over the top and serve, cut into wedges.

Serves 4.

— BLACKBERRY APPLE STACK —

eight 17.5 cm (7 in) crêpes, see pages 12-15
500 g (1 lb) cooking apples
375 g (12 oz) blackberries
60 g (2 oz/¼ cup) sugar
2 egg whites
125 g (4 oz/½ cup) caster sugar

Keep crêpes warm while preparing filling. Peel, core and roughly chop the apples. Put into a saucepan with blackberries and sugar, and simmer over low heat until fruit is soft. Set aside for 10 minutes to cool.

Put one crêpe on large ovenproof serving plate and spread with some filling. Top with a second crêpe and repeat until all the crêpes and filling are used, finishing with a crêpe.

Preheat oven to 230C (450F/Gas 8). In a bowl, whisk egg whites to stiff peaks, then fold in caster sugar. Cover top and sides of crêpes with meringue and bake in the oven for 2 minutes, until pale golden. Serve at once, cut into wedges.

Serves 4.

— FRENCH CHESTNUT CRÊPES —

eight 17.5 cm (7 in) crêpes, see pages 12-15

250 g (8 oz) can sweetened chestnut purée

90 ml (3 fl oz/generous ⅓ cup) orange juice

3 teaspoons lemon juice

3 teaspoons white rum

30 g (1 oz/6 teaspoons) butter, melted

3 teaspoons icing sugar

Preheat oven to 150C (300F/Gas 2). Spread each crêpe with chestnut purée and fold into quarters. Place in a shallow flameproof dish. Mix together the orange juice, lemon juice and rum and pour over crêpes. Cover loosely with foil and heat through in the oven for 30 minutes.

Remove foil. Brush crêpes with butter and sprinkle with icing sugar, then put under a hot grill for 2 minutes, or until glazed. Serve at once.

Serves 4.

CRÊPES SUZETTE

eight 17.5 cm (7 in) crêpes, see pages 12-15

90 g (3 oz/⅓ cup) unsalted butter

90 g (3 oz/½ cup) icing sugar

9 teaspoons orange juice

3 teaspoons lemon juice

6 teaspoons orange-flavoured liqueur

3 teaspoons brandy

orange slices and bay leaves, to garnish

Fold each crêpe in quarters. Put butter, icing sugar, orange juice and lemon juice into a large frying pan and heat gently until the butter has melted and the mixture is syrupy. Stir in the liqueur.

Put the crêpes in the pan and turn once so they are covered in sauce. Pour over the brandy and quickly light with a match. Serve as soon as the flames die down, garnished with orange slices and bay leaves.

Serves 4.

— LEMON MERINGUE LAYER —

eight 17.5 cm (7 in) crêpes, see pages 12-15

1 quantity Fresh Lemon Topping, see page 36

2 egg whites

125 g (4 oz/½ cup) caster sugar

15 g (½ oz/2 tablespoons) whole blanched almonds

angelica 'leaves', to decorate

Keep crêpes warm while preparing lemon topping. Put one crêpe on a large ovenproof serving plate. Spread with some lemon topping. Top with a second crêpe and repeat until all the crêpes and the topping are used, finishing with a crêpe.

Preheat oven to 230C (450F/Gas 8). Whisk egg whites to stiff peaks, then fold in caster sugar. Cover top and sides of crêpes with meringue. Top with almonds and bake in the oven for 2 minutes, until pale golden. Decorate with angelica 'leaves', then serve at once, cut into wedges.

Serves 4.

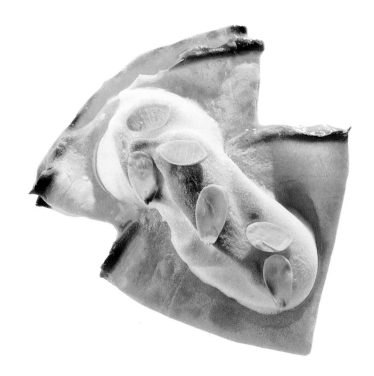

APRICOT DELIGHT

eight 17.5 cm (7 in) crêpes, see pages
12-15

375 g (12 oz/3 cups) dried apricots,
chopped and soaked overnight

90 g (3 oz/⅓ cup) sugar

finely grated peel and juice of 1 lemon

2 egg whites

125 g (4 oz/½ cup) caster sugar

15 g (½ oz/6 teaspoons) flaked
almonds

Keep crêpes warm while preparing
filling. Drain the apricots and put
into a saucepan with the sugar and
just enough water to cover, then
simmer until soft. Push through a
sieve or purée in a blender or food
processor. Stir the lemon peel and
juice into the apricot purée.

Preheat oven to 190C (375F/Gas
5). Put a little of the mixture on
each crêpe and fold in quarters.
Arrange in a single layer in a shallow
ovenproof serving dish, cover with
foil and heat through in the oven
for 30 minutes.

In a bowl, whisk egg whites to stiff
peaks, then fold in caster sugar.
Remove foil from crêpes and spoon
the meringue over to cover all or
part of crêpes, then sprinkle with
almonds. Put under a hot grill for 2
minutes, until lightly browned.
Serve at once.

Serves 4.

— ORANGE LIQUEUR GÂTEAU —

eight 17.5 cm (7 in) crêpes, see pages 12-15

250 g (8 oz) can mandarin oranges

2 teaspoons cornflour

3 teaspoons clear honey

3 teaspoons apricot jam

9 teaspoons orange-flavoured liqueur

155 ml (5 fl oz/⅔ cup) whipping cream

Keep crêpes warm while preparing filling. Drain oranges well, reserving the juice, then set aside. Mix cornflour with 3 teaspoons juice and put remaining juice into a saucepan with honey and jam. Bring to the boil and add cornflour mixture, then stir over low heat until thick and clear. Stir in 6 teaspoons liqueur.

Put one crêpe on a serving plate. Arrange a few mandarin oranges on top and sprinkle with the honey mixture. Put on a second crêpe and repeat until all the crêpes, oranges and liqueur-flavoured mixture are used, finishing with a crêpe. Arrange any remaining mandarin oranges on top.

In a bowl, whip cream to soft peaks and fold in remaining liqueur. Put cream in a serving bowl.

Serve the crêpe and orange gâteau cut into wedges, with the cream handed separately.

Serves 4.

Variation: Add 2 or 3 sliced kiwi fruit with the oranges, then pipe rosettes of cream and decorate with pieces of fruit.

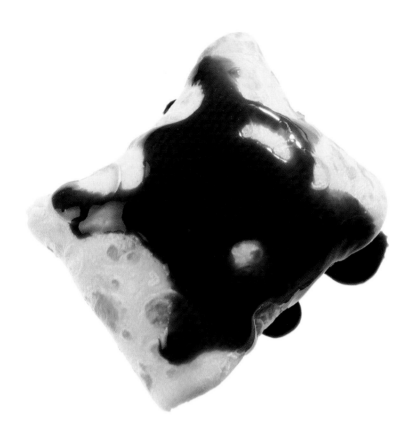

ICE CREAM CRÊPES

eight 17.5 cm (7 in) crêpes, see pages 12-15
625 ml (20 fl oz) block vanilla ice cream
6 teaspoons cherry brandy
CHOCOLATE SAUCE:
125 g (4 oz/½ cup) caster sugar
60 g (2 oz/½ cup) cocoa

To make the chocolate sauce, put 155 ml (5 fl oz/⅔ cup) water and the sugar into a saucepan and stir over low heat until sugar has dissolved. Bring to boil, then simmer for 1 minute. Add cocoa and return to the boil, beating until smooth. Set aside and keep warm.

Cut ice cream into 8 cubes and wrap each one in a crêpe, then put two crêpes on to each plate. Sprinkle with cherry brandy and serve at once with hot chocolate sauce spooned over.

Serves 4.

APPLE & RUM CRÊPES

eight 17.5 cm (7 in) crêpes, see pages 12-15

250 g (8 oz) cream cheese

1 eating apple, peeled, cored and sliced

125 g (4 oz/¾ cup) sultanas

apple slices sprinkled with brown sugar, to decorate

RUM SAUCE:

60 g (2 oz/¼ cup) unsalted butter

125 g (4 oz/¾ cup) moist brown sugar

3 tablespoons whipping cream

60 ml (2 fl oz/¼ cup) dark rum

To make rum sauce, put butter and sugar into a bowl, beat until soft and creamy, then work in the cream and rum. Turn into a serving bowl and set aside.

Meanwhile, keep crêpes warm while preparing filling. Put the cheese into a bowl and beat until light and fluffy, then stir in apple slices and sultanas. Divide mixture between crêpes and lightly roll up each. Place in a single layer on a serving dish and decorate with the apple slices. Serve with the sauce for pouring over.

Serves 4.

VIENNESE CRÊPES

eight 17.5 cm (7 in) crêpes, see pages 12-15

90 g (3 oz/⅓ cup) unsalted butter

90 g (3 oz/½ cup) icing sugar

30 g (1 oz/¼ cup) ground almonds

3 teaspoons coffee essence

1 quantity Chocolate Sauce, see page 65

Make chocolate sauce and keep warm. Keep the crêpes warm while preparing the filling. Put the butter into a bowl and beat until light and fluffy, then add the sugar, almonds and coffee essence, beating well until light and creamy.

Divide coffee mixture between crêpes and fold into quarters. Place 2 crêpes on each plate and serve with hot chocolate sauce for pouring over.

Serves 4.

BASIC WAFFLES

185 g (6 oz/1½ cups) plain flour
2 teaspoons baking powder
½ teaspoon salt
2 teaspoons sugar
2 eggs, separated
250 ml (8 fl oz/1 cup) milk
90 g (3 oz/⅓ cup) butter, melted
TO SERVE:
butter and maple syrup, or bacon

Sift flour, baking powder and salt into a bowl, then stir in sugar. Put egg yolks, milk and butter into a separate bowl and beat well, then add to dry ingredients. Beat hard to combine. Whisk egg whites in a bowl to stiff peaks and fold into the other ingredients.

Heat waffle iron, but do not grease. To test for correct heat, put 1 teaspoon water inside waffle iron, close and heat. When steaming stops, heat is correct.

Put 3 teaspoons batter into centre of each compartment, close and cook until puffed up and golden brown. Lift out waffles with a fork, set aside and keep warm, then continue until all the batter is used. Serve hot with butter and maple syrup, or bacon.

Makes 6.

Variation: Serve the waffles sandwiched together with whipped cream. Decorate with soft fruit and icing sugar.

—— CRISPY CHEESE WAFFLES ——

185 g (6 oz/1½ cups) plain flour

2 teaspoons baking powder

½ teaspoon salt

2 eggs, separated

250 ml (8 fl oz/1 cup) milk

90 g (3 oz/⅓ cup) butter, melted

60 g (2 oz/½ cup) grated Cheddar cheese

TO SERVE:

cream cheese and sliced eating apples, and crisp grilled bacon

Sift flour, baking powder and salt into a bowl. Put egg yolks, milk and butter into a bowl and beat well. Add to dry ingredients with cheese, and beat hard to combine. Whisk egg whites in a bowl to stiff peaks and fold into other ingredients.

Heat waffle iron, but do not grease. Put 3 teaspoons batter into centre of each compartment, close and cook until puffed up and golden brown. Lift out waffles with a fork, set aside and keep warm, then continue until all the batter is used. Serve hot with cream cheese, sliced eating apples and with crisp, grilled bacon.

Makes 6.

– CHOCOLATE CREAM WAFFLES –

185 g (6 oz/1½ cups) plain flour
2 teaspoons baking powder
½ teaspoon salt
30 g (1 oz/6 teaspoons) sugar
60 g (2 oz) plain (dark) chocolate
2 eggs, separated
250 ml (8 fl oz/1 cup) milk
90 g (3 oz/⅓ cup) butter, melted
few drops vanilla essence
TO SERVE:
155 ml (5 fl oz/⅔ cup) whipping cream
grated chocolate

Sift flour, baking powder and salt into a bowl, then stir in sugar. Melt chocolate in the top of a double boiler or a bowl set over a saucepan of simmering water.

Put egg yolks, milk, butter and chocolate into a bowl with the vanilla essence and beat well. Add to dry ingredients and beat hard to combine. Whisk egg whites in a bowl to stiff peaks and fold into other ingredients.

Heat waffle iron, but do not grease. Put 3 teaspoons batter into centre of each compartment. Close and cook until puffed up and crisp. Lift out waffles with a fork, set aside and keep warm, then continue until all the batter is used. Whip cream to soft peaks in a bowl. Serve hot waffles with cream piped on top or in bowl for spooning over. Decorate with grated chocolate.

Makes 6.

—— BANANA NUT WAFFLES ——

185 g (6 oz/1½ cups) plain flour
2 teaspoons baking powder
½ teaspoon salt
2 teaspoons sugar
2 eggs, separated
250 ml (8 fl oz/1 cup) milk
90 g (3 oz/½ cup) butter, melted
90 g (3 oz/¾ cup) walnuts, finely chopped
2 bananas
30 g (1 oz/2 tablespoons) icing sugar
3 teaspoons lemon juice

Sift flour, baking powder and salt into a bowl, then stir in sugar. Put egg yolks, milk and butter into a bowl and beat well, then add to dry ingredients and beat hard to combine. Stir in 3 teaspoons of the chopped walnuts.

Whisk egg whites in a bowl to stiff peaks and fold into other ingredients.

Heat waffle iron, but do not grease. Put 3 teaspoons batter into centre of each compartment, close and cook until puffed up and golden brown. Lift out waffles with a fork, set aside and keep warm in a low oven, then continue until all the batter is used.

While waffles are cooking, peel and slice bananas into a bowl with icing sugar and lemon juice. Serve the hot waffles topped with banana slices and sprinkle over remaining walnuts.

Makes 6.

— APRICOT CREAM WAFFLES —

6 Basic Waffles, see pages 68

220 g (7 oz) can apricots in syrup

3 tablespoons dark orange marmalade

3 teaspoons brandy

60 g (2 oz/½ cup) flaked almonds

TO SERVE:

155 ml (5 fl oz/⅔ cup) whipping cream

While the waffles are cooking, prepare the topping. Put apricots with their syrup, marmalade and brandy into a blender or food processor and blend to a smooth purée. Put into a serving bowl and set aside.

Put the almonds on a baking sheet and place under a medium grill for 2–3 minutes, stirring occasionally with a long-handled spoon, until golden. Whip cream in a bowl to soft peaks.

Serve the hot waffles with a topping of apricot purée, sprinkled with toasted nuts and the whipped cream in a separate bowl.

Serves 6.

– STRAWBERRY RUM WAFFLES –

6 Basic Waffles, see page 68
250 g (8 oz) strawberries, hulled and thickly sliced
60 g (2 oz/¼ cup) caster sugar
6 teaspoons white rum
6 scoops strawberry ice cream

While the waffles are cooking, prepare the topping. Put the strawberries into a bowl with the sugar and rum, stir well and leave to stand until waffles are ready.

Spoon strawberries and their soaking liquid over hot waffles, then top each one with a scoop of ice cream. Serve at once.

Serves 6.

Note: Orange juice makes an excellent substitute for the rum, if desired.

OMELETTE TECHNIQUES

There are three basic types of omelette cooked over heat, although they may be adapted for baking in the oven or cooking in a microwave oven.

The French omelette, also called a plain omelette, is like a thick soft golden pillow, which may be flavoured or filled.

The soufflé omelette is also known as a fluffy or puffy omelette. It is made by beating egg yolks separately and then folding in stiffy-whisked egg whites. This results in a light soufflé-style mixture, which collapses quickly, and is most often used for sweet omelettes.

The Spanish omelette (tortilla) is a thick omelette with vegetable and/or meat, poultry or fish cooked in the beaten eggs. This omelette is not folded, but, instead, cut into wedges for serving.

Ingredients

An omelette simply consists of beaten eggs cooked in butter. Eggs weighing 60 g (2 oz) are the best to use, and a 3-egg omelette is enough for one person, but with a substantial filling may be made to serve two people. A 5–6 egg omelette will serve two people, but a filling will extend the egg mixture to serve three.

If 1 teaspoon water is added to each egg, the omelette will be light, but this is not necessary. Milk should not be added as this makes the egg mixture heavier. For cooking, 15 g ($\frac{1}{2}$ oz/3 teaspoons) butter is usual for a 3-egg omelette.

Flavourings and fillings

The rich mixture of fresh eggs and butter needs no more flavouring than salt and pepper, but chopped fresh herbs may be added, allowing 3 teaspoons herbs to 3 eggs. Cheese may also be used, allowing 60 g (2 oz/$\frac{1}{2}$ cup) cheese to 3 eggs.

Flavourings such as grated cheese, chopped ham or cream cheese may be folded into a plain omelette, or fillings such as mushrooms or bacon may be cooked in a little butter before being folded into the omelette. Fish, shellfish, poultry, game or ham may be added to a white sauce to use as a filling. Soufflé omelettes may be filled with fruit or any of the sweet crêpe toppings.

Basic preparation and serving

Always use fresh ingredients, and only prepare an omelette just before serving. Break the eggs into a bowl and beat lightly with a fork, not a whisk – the eggs should be just broken and mixed together. If eggs are over-beaten, a thin watery omelette results.

Before cooking, warm the serving plates, and preheat the oven or grill if necessary. Put the pan over low heat to become thoroughly hot, then put the butter into the pan and when sizzling but not brown pour in the egg mixture.

Using a fork or spatula, draw the mixture from the sides to the middle of the pan, allowing the uncooked egg to run underneath and cook quickly. Repeat this process two or three times so all the egg sets and is raised up and fluffy, not flat. Only cook for about 2 minutes, until the base is light golden-brown and the top still slightly runny, then remove from heat.

If filling an omelette, make a little cut on each side of the cooked mixture. Put filling on one half, fold omelette in half and lift onto a warm plate. The filling should be pre-cooked and warm.

To fold a plain omelette, fold over one-third of cooked mixture away from handle, using a palette knife. Place over a warm plate and hold the handle of the pan with the palm of your hand uppermost. Shake the omelette to the edge of the pan and tip completely over to make another fold. If liked, quickly drop a piece of butter on top of the hot omelette and spread over surface to give an attractive glaze.

Spanish omelettes, or those with a lot of filling in sauce, may be served flat and cut into wedges. They may be placed under a grill to set the top or lightly brown the filling.

Baked and microwaved omelettes
Omelettes may be baked for about 10–15 minutes in a moderate oven, and this is a good method for a filled omelette which will be served flat. An omelette pan with an ovenproof handle is best to use, as the base of the omelette should be lightly cooked over heat before finishing in the oven.

Omelettes may be successfully cooked in a microwave oven. For a 3-egg omelette, melt the butter for 30 seconds in a shallow 17.5 cm (7 in) microwave dish before the eggs are poured in, then add the beaten eggs and cook for 1 minute on high. Lift eggs from sides with a fork, then continue microwaving for 1 minute on high.

Omelette fondante
A very rich plain omelette may be made by adding 3 teaspoons single (light) cream and 3 teaspoons flaked butter to the beaten eggs. As the omelette cooks, the butter melts into little pockets to give extra flavour and richness.

BASIC OMELETTE

3 eggs
salt and pepper
15 g (½ oz/3 teaspoons) butter
watercress sprig and tomato slice,
to garnish

In a bowl, beat eggs with salt and pepper to taste until just mixed. Put omelette pan over low heat to become thoroughly hot.

Put butter into pan. When butter is sizzling but not brown, pour in eggs. Using a fork or spatula, draw mixture from sides to middle of pan, allowing uncooked egg to run underneath. Repeat 2 or 3 times so egg is pushed up lightly and becomes fluffy. Cook for about 2 minutes, until golden-brown underneath and the top is still slightly runny.

Using a palette knife, fold over one-third of mixture away from handle. Hold over a warm serving plate, with the palm of your hand uppermost. Shake the omelette to the edge of the pan and tip completely over to make another fold. Garnish with watercress and tomato slice and serve at once.

Serves 1.

– SMOKED SALMON OMELETTES –

6 eggs
salt and pepper
30 g (1 oz/6 teaspoons) butter
125 g (4 oz) smoked salmon, finely chopped
1 teaspoon chopped fresh parsley
1 teaspoon chopped fresh chives
fresh chives and smoked salmon, to garnish

In a bowl, beat eggs with salt and pepper to taste. Put omelette pan over low heat to become throughly hot. Melt a little butter in pan, then pour in 6 teaspoons egg and cook until just set. Lift onto a baking sheet and keep warm. Repeat until all the eggs are used.

Mix the smoked salmon with parsley and chives and spoon onto one side of each small omelette. Fold over, garnish with chives and smoked salmon and serve at once.

Serves 4.

—PRAWN SOUFFLÉ OMELETTE—

3 eggs, separated
salt and pepper
30 g (1 oz/6 teaspoons) butter
125 g (4 oz) peeled cooked prawns, thawed if frozen
3 teaspoons lemon juice
1 teaspoon chilli sauce
lemon slice and fresh fennel sprig, to garnish

In a bowl, beat egg yolks with salt and pepper to taste. In a separate bowl, whisk whites to stiff peaks and fold into yolks.

Melt half butter in a 17.5 cm (7 in) omelette pan. Pour in mixture and cook over low heat for 2–3 minutes, until base is set and golden brown.

While omelette is cooking, prepare filling. Put prawns, lemon juice, chilli sauce and remaining butter into a small pan and heat through. Put omelette under high grill for 30 seconds, until lightly browned, then spoon filling over half of the omelette and fold over. Cut in half, garnish with lemon slice and fresh fennel sprig and serve at once.

Serves 2.

CURRIED OMELETTE

one 3-egg Basic Omelette, see page 76
1 onion, finely chopped
30 g (1 oz/6 teaspoons) butter
2 teaspoons curry powder
1 eating apple, peeled, cored and finely diced
3 teaspoons mango chutney, finely chopped
salt and pepper
squeeze of lemon juice
apple slices and fresh coriander sprigs, to garnish

Prepare filling before making omelette. Put onion into a frying pan with butter and cook over low heat for 3 minutes. Stir in curry powder and apple and continue cooking over low heat for 5 minutes, then stir in chutney and season to taste with salt and pepper and lemon juice.

Make omelette and spoon curry mixture over half the egg mixture. Fold omelette over and cut in half to serve. Garnish with a few apple slices and fresh coriander sprigs.

Serves 2.

– ARNOLD BENNETT OMELETTE –

3 eggs
185 g (6 oz) smoked haddock fillets, cooked, skinned and flaked
salt and pepper
30 g (1 oz/6 teaspoons) butter
75 ml (2½ fl oz/⅓ cup) single (light) cream
60 g (2 oz/½ cup) grated Cheddar cheese
lemon twist and chopped fresh parsley, to garnish

In a bowl, beat eggs lightly, then stir in fish and season to taste with salt and pepper.

Melt butter in a 17.5 cm (7 in) omelette pan. Pour in egg mixture and cook over medium heat, drawing cooked egg from edge of pan towards middle, until just set. Lift onto a warm flameproof serving plate with a palette knife.

Cover omelette with cream and sprinkle with cheese. Put under a medium grill until golden and bubbling. Do not fold, but garnish and serve at once cut in half.

Serves 2.

ITALIAN OMELETTE

60 g (2 oz/¼ cup) butter
1 small onion, finely chopped
1 tomato, skinned and chopped
1 tablespoon chopped green pepper (capsicum)
3 eggs
60 g (2 oz/⅓ cup) cooked pasta, well drained
salt and pepper
6 teaspoons grated Parmesan cheese
fresh basil sprig, to garnish

Prepare filling before making omelette. Melt half butter in a small saucepan, add onion and cook over low heat for 2 minutes. Stir in tomato and pepper (capsicum), cover and cook over low heat for 10 minutes.

In a bowl, beat eggs and stir in pasta with salt and pepper. Melt remaining butter in a 17.5 cm (7 in) omelette pan. Pour in mixture and cook over low heat, drawing cooked egg from edge of pan towards middle until just set.

Spread filling over half of the omelette and fold over. Sprinkle with cheese and put under hot grill for 30 seconds to melt the cheese. Cut in half, garnish with basil and serve at once.

Serves 1.

— CHICKEN LIVER OMELETTE —

125 g (4 oz) chicken livers, thawed if frozen and roughly chopped
1 small onion, finely chopped
15 g (½ oz/3 teaspoons) butter
2 teaspoons chopped fresh thyme
1 teaspoon plain flour
6 teaspoons chicken stock
salt and pepper
one 3-egg Basic Omelette, see page 76
fresh thyme sprigs and grapes, to garnish

Prepare filling before making omelette. Put chicken livers and onion into a small saucepan with butter and cook over low heat for 3 minutes, stirring, until onion is golden. Stir in thyme, flour and stock. Bring to the boil, season to taste with salt and pepper and simmer for 10 minutes.

Make omelette and spoon over chicken liver filling. Fold omelette over. Garnish with thyme sprigs and grapes and serve at once.

Serves 1.

—— FLORENTINE OMELETTE ——

125 g (4 oz) fresh spinach
½ quantity Cheese Sauce, see page 23
one 3-egg Basic Omelette, see page 76
60 g (2 oz/½ cup) grated Cheddar cheese
cayenne pepper for sprinkling

Prepare filling before making omelette. Wash the spinach very well, drain and put into a saucepan with only the water clinging to its leaves. Cover and cook over low heat until spinach has shrunk and is very tender. Drain well and press out excess moisture. Set aside. Warm through sauce and keep warm.

Make omelette and fill with spinach. Fold over and lift onto warm flameproof serving plate. Spoon over cheese sauce and sprinkle on the grated cheese. Put under hot grill until sauce is bubbling and golden, sprinkle with cayenne pepper and serve at once.

Serves 1.

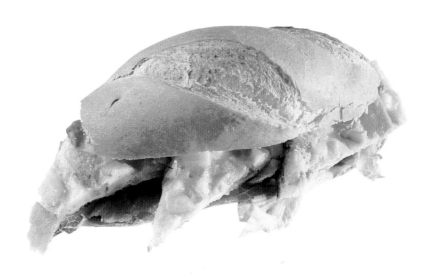

TORTILLA LOAVES

4 lean rashers bacon, rinds removed and chopped
15 g (½ oz/3 teaspoons) butter
250 g (8 oz) cooked potatoes, diced
6 eggs
salt and pepper
4 long bread rolls
butter for spreading
lettuce leaves

Put bacon into a frying pan with butter and fry quickly until fat runs. Stir in potatoes and cook over medium heat until golden.

In a bowl, beat eggs with salt and pepper to taste, then pour over potatoes and cook over medium heat, lifting with a fork, until just set.

Split rolls lengthwise and lightly spread cut sides with butter. Place a lettuce leaf on bottom half of each roll. Cut egg mixture into slices, then place on lettuce and top with upper slices of rolls. Serve hot or cold.

Serves 4.

– GARLIC CROÛTON OMELETTE –

30 g (1 oz/6 teaspoons) butter
3 teaspoons oil
1 clove garlic, crushed
1 medium slice white bread, crusts removed and cut into 1 cm (½ in) cubes
salt and pepper
one 3-egg Basic Omelette, see page 76
celery leaves and extra croûtons, to garnish

Prepare garlic croûtons before making omelette. Heat butter and oil in a frying pan and stir in garlic. Add bread cubes and fry until crisp and golden. Drain well on absorbent kitchen paper and season to taste with salt and pepper.

Make omelette and sprinkle croûtons on half of the omelette. Fold omelette over, garnish with celery leaves and croûtons and serve at once.

Serves 1.

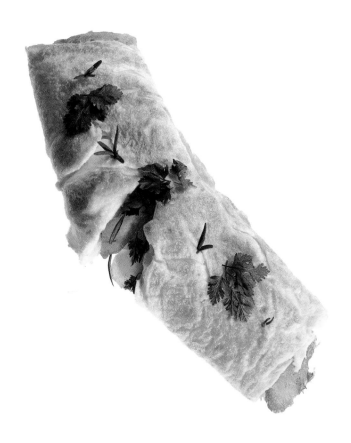

— POTATO & HERB OMELETTE —

3 teaspoons vegetable oil
1 large potato, cooked and thinly sliced
1 teaspoon chopped fresh rosemary
1 teaspoon chopped fresh chervil
salt and pepper
one 3-egg Basic Omelette, see page 76
fresh rosemary and chervil sprigs, to garnish

Prepare filling before making omelette. Heat the oil in a frying pan, add the potato slices in a single layer and fry until crisp and golden. Drain well on absorbent kitchen paper.

Mix potatoes with rosemary and chervil and season well with salt and pepper. Keep warm.

Make omelette and put potato mixture on half of the omelette. Fold omelette over, garnish with rosemary and chervil and serve at once.

Serves 1.

—— HAM & HERB OMELETTE ——

60 g (2 oz) cooked ham, finely chopped
1 small bunch watercress leaves,
finely chopped
15 g (½ oz/3 teaspoons) butter
salt and pepper
one 3-egg Basic Omelette, see page 76
fresh watercress sprig and ham rolls, to
garnish

Prepare filling before making omelette. Put ham and watercress leaves into a small saucepan with butter and shake over low heat for 1 minute to warm through. Remove from heat and season well with salt and pepper.

Make omelette and spoon ham mixture over half of the omelette. Fold over, garnish and serve.

Serves 1.

Note: If fresh watercress isn't available, substitute chopped fresh parsley or chives, or 2 finely chopped spring onions.

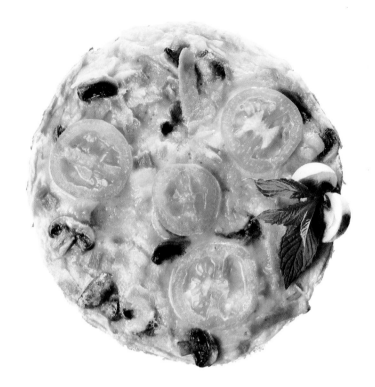

——— BREAKFAST OMELETTE ———

2 lean rashers bacon, rinded and finely chopped
15 g (½ oz/3 teaspoons) butter
60 g (2 oz) mushrooms, thinly sliced
3 eggs
salt and pepper
1 tomato, skinned and sliced
fresh mint sprig and halved mushroom, to garnish

Put bacon into a 17.5 cm (7 in) omelette pan with butter and cook over low heat for 2 minutes. Stir in mushrooms and continue cooking over low heat for 2 minutes.

In a bowl, beat eggs with salt and pepper to taste, then pour into pan and top with tomato slices. As eggs cook, draw the mixture from edge of pan to centre so that liquid egg runs to base of pan. When top is just set, slide omelette flat on to serving plate. Garnish with a mint sprig and halved mushroom and serve at once.

Serves 1.

— FLUFFY CHEESE OMELETTE —

3 eggs, separated
salt and pepper
15 g (½ oz/3 teaspoons) butter
60 g (2 oz/½ cup) grated Red Leicester cheese or other red cheese
fresh chervil sprigs, to garnish

In a bowl, beat egg yolks with salt and pepper to taste until creamy. Whisk whites to stiff peaks in a separate bowl and fold into yolks. Melt butter in a 17.5 cm (7 in) omelette pan, pour in egg mixture and cook over low heat for 2-3 minutes, until base is set and golden-brown.

Lift omelette on to a warm flame-proof plate. Sprinkle three-quarters of the cheese over surface and fold omelette in half, then sprinkle remaining cheese on top. Put under hot grill for 30 seconds, to melt cheese. Garnish with chervil, then serve at once.

Serves 1.

— BASIC SOUFFLÉ OMELETTE —

3 eggs, separated
3 teaspoons caster sugar
15 g (½ oz/3 teaspoons) butter
FILLING:
Sweet filling, see pages 28-37

In a bowl, beat egg yolks and sugar until thick, pale and creamy. Whisk egg whites to stiff peaks and fold into yolks.

Put butter into a 17.5 cm (7 in) omelette pan and melt over moderate heat, pour in egg mixture and lightly level the surface. Cook over low heat until bottom is set and pale

golden-brown, then put omelette under medium grill until top is lightly browned.

Spread filling on half omelette. Fold over and serve at once.

Serves 2.

Variation: Use a little hot jam, marmalade or honey, which may be mixed with finely chopped nuts, for the filling. Alternatively, fill omelette with sliced fresh fruit, lightly sweetened and flavoured with liqueur.

— DIJON SURPRISE OMELETTE —

6 eggs
6 teaspoons caster sugar
2 almond macaroon biscuits, crushed
6 teaspoons single (light) cream
30 g (1 oz/6 teaspoons) butter
5 tablespoons blackcurrant jam
30 g (1 oz/¼ cup) finely chopped walnuts
TOPPING:
2 egg whites
125 g (4 oz/½ cup) caster sugar
6 teaspoons icing sugar, sifted

Preheat oven to 220C (425F/Gas 7). In a bowl, beat eggs, sugar, crushed biscuits and cream until thick and creamy. Melt half the butter in a 17.5 cm (7 in) omelette pan, pour in half egg mixture and cook over low heat until just set. Lift on to a warm ovenproof plate, then repeat with remaining egg mixture.

Warm jam in a small saucepan and stir in walnuts. Spread mixture on first omelette and top with other omelette. In a bowl, whisk egg whites to stiff peaks, then fold in caster sugar. Carefully pipe or spread over omelettes, making sure they are completely covered. Sprinkle with icing sugar and bake in the oven for 3 minutes, until meringue is lightly coloured. Serve at once.

Serves 4.

—— CHRISTMAS OMELETTE ——

6 eggs, separated
6 teaspoons caster sugar
grated peel of 1 orange
60 ml (2 fl oz/¼ cup) white rum
30 g (1 oz/6 teaspoons) butter
6 tablespoons fruit mincemeat
2 teaspoons icing sugar, sifted
holly leaves, to decorate

In a bowl, beat egg yolks with sugar, orange peel and 3 teaspoons rum. Whisk whites to stiff peaks and fold into yolks.

Melt butter in a 20 cm (8 in) omelette pan, pour in mixture and cook over low heat for 4–5 minutes, until golden-brown underneath.

Warm fruit mincemeat in a saucepan until lukewarm, then spread on half omelette and fold omelette over. Lift onto a warm flameproof serving plate and sprinkle with icing sugar. Place under hot grill for 30 seconds, to melt sugar and glaze.

Put remaining rum into a small saucepan and warm gently, then pour over omelette and ignite at once with a match. Serve as soon as flames die down, decorated with holly leaves.

Serves 3–4.

– SUMMER SOUFFLÉ OMELETTE –

185 g (6 oz) prepared soft fruits, such as blackcurrants, redcurrants, raspberries, strawberries
3 tablespoons crème de cassis or water
3 teaspoons caster sugar
3 teaspoons arrowroot
one 3-egg Basic Soufflé Omelette, see page 90
1 tablespoon icing sugar, sifted
soft fruit and leaves, to decorate

Prepare filling before making omelette. Put fruit in a saucepan with crème de cassis or water and sugar. Heat gently until juices run. Remove from heat. Mix arrowroot with a little water and stir in. Return to heat and cook, stirring, until thick. Leave filling to cool.

Make omelette and place on a warm serving plate. Spoon fruit mixture over half omelette and fold over, then sprinkle with icing sugar. Decorate with soft fruit and leaves, if desired, and serve at once.

Serves 2.

PINEAPPLE OMELETTE

220 g (7 oz) can pineapple pieces
in natural juice

1 teaspoon arrowroot

2 teaspoons finely grated lemon peel

2 teaspoons chopped fresh mint

one 3-egg Basic Soufflé Omelette,
see page 90

lemon twist and fresh mint sprig,
to decorate

Prepare filling before making omelette. Drain pineapple pieces, reserving juice. Put 9 teaspoons pineapple juice into a saucepan and bring to the boil. Mix arrowroot with 2 teaspoons water, stir into juice and heat gently until mixture is slightly thickened and clear. Finely chop pineapple and stir into pan with lemon peel and chopped mint.

Make omelette and lift onto warm serving plate. Spoon pineapple sauce over half omelette and fold omelette over. Garnish with a lemon twist and fresh mint sprig and serve at once.

Serves 2.

— BAKED ALASKA OMELETTE —

625 ml (20 fl oz) block vanilla ice cream	
250 g (8 oz) raspberries or strawberries	
6 teaspoons kirsch	
6 teaspoons caster sugar	
3 eggs, separated	
one 17.5 cm (7 in) oblong sponge cake	
caster sugar for sprinkling.	
strawberry halves, to decorate	

Make sure ice cream is very hard before preparing recipe. Preheat oven to 220C (425F/Gas 7).

Leave raspberries whole, or slice strawberries, if using. Put into a bowl with kirsch and half sugar and leave to stand while preparing recipe.

Beat egg yolks with remaining sugar until thick and creamy. Whisk whites to stiff peaks and fold into yolks.

Place sponge cake on a large ovenproof serving plate. Spoon over fruit and soaking liquid and top with block of ice cream, cutting the ice cream to fit, if necessary.

Quickly cover ice cream and sponge cake with egg mixture, making sure the top and sides are completely covered. Sprinkle with caster sugar and bake for 3 minutes, until light golden. Decorate with strawberry halves, then serve at once, cut into wedges.

Serves 6.

— BERRY SOUFFLÉ OMELETTE —

3 eggs, separated
6 teaspoons caster sugar
125 g (4 oz) blackberries
45 g (1½ oz/9 teaspoons) butter
leaves, to decorate
TO SERVE:
155 ml (5 fl oz/⅔ cup) whipping cream

In a bowl, beat egg yolks and half sugar until thick and creamy. Whisk whites to stiff peaks and fold into yolks.

Melt 30 g (1 oz/6 teaspoons) butter in a 17.5 cm (7 in) omelette pan, pour in mixture and cook over low heat for 2–3 minutes, until base is golden-brown.

While omelette is cooking, put blackberries into a saucepan with remaining butter and sugar and simmer for 2 minutes. Put omelette under medium grill until top is lightly browned.

Lift omelette onto a warm serving dish and spoon over berries. Decorate with leaves. In a bowl, whip cream to soft peaks and pipe over or serve separately to spoon over each serving. Serve omelette at once.

Serves 2.

Note: When blackberries are unavailable use raspberries or hulled strawberries.

—— FLUFFY FRUIT OMELETTE ——

2 eating apples, peeled, cored and diced

1 banana, thinly sliced

1 orange, peeled, thinly sliced and quartered

3 eggs, separated

6 teaspoons caster sugar

15 g (½ oz/3 teaspoons) butter

2 teaspoons icing sugar, sifted

orange segments and fresh mint leaves, to decorate

Put apples, banana and orange into a bowl. Put egg yolks and sugar into a bowl and beat until pale and creamy, then stir in the fruit. Whisk egg whites to stiff peaks and fold in the sugar. Fold into fruit mixture.

Melt butter in a 20 cm (8 in) omelette pan, pour in mixture and cook over low heat for 2–3 minutes, until base is golden-brown. Put under medium grill until top is lightly browned.

Sprinkle with icing sugar and cut into quarters. Decorate with orange segments and fresh mint leaves. Serve straight from pan, using a fish slice or wide palette knife, as omelette breaks easily.

Serves 4.

– CHERRY SOUFFLÉ OMELETTE –

60 g (2 oz/¼ cup) sugar
125 g (4 oz) black cherries, stoned and halved
3 eggs, separated
6 teaspoons caster sugar
15 g (½ oz/3 teaspoons) butter

Prepare filling before making omelette. Put the sugar and 155 ml (5 fl oz/⅔ cup) water into a small saucepan and heat gently until the sugar has dissolved. Bring to the boil, add cherries and cook for 3 minutes, until just soft.

In a bowl, beat egg yolks with half caster sugar. Whisk whites to stiff peaks in a separate bowl, then fold into the beaten yolks.

Melt butter in a 17.5 cm (7 in) omelette pan, pour in egg mixture and cook over low heat, loosening edges, until fluffy and lightly browned underneath. Put under medium grill until top is lightly browned. Spread cherries and half the syrup over the omelette and fold omelette in half. Lift onto a serving plate and sprinkle with remaining sugar. Serve at once.

Serves 2.

Note: Save the leftover syrup to spoon over ice cream.

— SWEET & SHARP OMELETTE —

6 eggs, separated
155 ml (5 fl oz/⅔ cup) thick sour cream
½ teaspoon finely grated lemon peel
2 teaspoons lemon juice
½ teaspoon salt
30 g (1 oz/6 teaspoons) butter
TOPPING:
2 teaspoons caster sugar, if desired
4 tablespoons cherry or strawberry jam
155 ml (5 fl oz/⅔ cup) thick sour cream

In a bowl, beat the egg yolks, sour cream, lemon peel and juice and salt until well mixed. Whisk egg whites to stiff peaks and fold into the yolks.

Melt butter in a 20 cm (8 in) omelette pan, pour in mixture and cook over low heat, loosening edges, until fluffy and lightly browned underneath.

Put under medium grill until top is lightly browned. To make topping, sprinkle with sugar, if desired, and cut into quarters, then serve each quarter with 1 tablespoon jam, topped with sour cream.

Serves 4.

FRIAR'S OMELETTE

60 g (2 oz/¼ cup) butter
2 medium slices white bread, crusts removed and cut into 1 cm (½ in) cubes
2 tomatoes, skinned and chopped
6 eggs
½ teaspoon chopped fresh mixed herbs
salt and pepper
whole chives, to garnish

Preheat oven to 160C (325F/Gas 3). Melt butter in a 20 cm (8 in) omelette pan with an ovenproof handle. Add bread cubes and fry over medium heat, stirring occasionally, until lightly browned all over, then add tomatoes and continue cooking for 1 minute. In a bowl, beat eggs with herbs and salt and pepper to taste.

Pour eggs into pan and cook for 1 minute, moving eggs from edge of pan to centre so liquid egg runs to base of pan.

Transfer to oven and cook for 10 minutes, until set. This omelette is good served hot or cold. Cut into wedges to serve and garnish with whole chives.

Serves 2–3.

– COTTAGE CHEESE OMELETTE –

4 eggs, separated
250 g (8 oz) cottage cheese
salt and pepper
30 g (1 oz/6 teaspoons) butter
2 tomatoes, skinned and sliced
fresh parsley sprigs, to garnish

Preheat oven to 160C (325F/Gas 3). In a bowl, beat egg yolks lightly, then add cottage cheese and salt and pepper to taste and beat well. In a separate bowl, whisk whites to stiff peaks and fold into egg mixture.

Melt butter in a 20 cm (8 in) omelette pan with an ovenproof handle. Pour in egg mixture, spreading lightly, and cook for 1 minute. Place tomato slices in a single layer on top of omelette, then transfer to oven and cook for 10 minutes, until set. Do not fold this omelette but, instead, serve cut in half. Serve at once, garnished with fresh parsley sprigs.

Serves 2.

— DEVILLED HAM OMELETTE —

5 eggs
½ teaspoon dry mustard
¼ teaspoon curry powder
salt and pepper
155 ml (5 fl oz/⅔ cup) thick sour cream
30 g (1 oz/6 teaspoons) butter
125 g (4 oz) cooked ham, finely chopped
fresh coriander sprigs, to garnish

Preheat oven to 160C (325F/Gas 3). In a bowl, beat eggs with mustard, curry powder and salt and pepper to taste. Add half the sour cream and 9 teaspoons water and beat until well mixed. Stir in half the cooked ham.

Melt butter in a 20 cm (8 in) omelette pan with an ovenproof handle. Pour in egg mixture and cook for 1 minute, moving eggs from edge of pan to centre so that liquid egg runs to base of pan. Transfer to oven and cook for 10 minutes, until set. Mix together remaining sour cream and ham and spoon over omelette. Serve at once, garnished with coriander sprigs.

Serves 2.

——— SUNDAY OMELETTE ———

1 chicken liver, thawed if frozen and roughly chopped
2 lean rashers bacon, rinds removed and finely chopped
1 small onion, finely chopped
60 g (2 oz/¼ cup) butter
1 large potato, cooked and diced
2 tablespoons cooked peas
4 eggs
salt and pepper
fresh parsley sprig and tomato slices, to garnish

Preheat oven to 160C (325F/Gas 3). Put chicken liver and bacon into a 20 cm (8 in) omelette pan with an ovenproof handle and cook over low heat until fat runs from bacon and liver is just coloured. Add onion and cook for 2–3 minutes, until lightly coloured. Add half the butter and the potato, and continue cooking until potato dice are golden. Stir in peas.

In a bowl, beat eggs with salt and pepper to taste. Add remaining butter to pan with vegetables, then pour in eggs and cook for 1 minute. Transfer to oven and cook for 10 minutes, until set. Do not fold this omelette but, instead, serve cut into pieces. Garnish with parsley and tomato slices and serve at once.

Serves 2–3.

— CHEESE SOUFFLÉ OMELETTE —

5 eggs, separated
salt and pepper
30 g (1 oz/6 teaspoons) butter
6 spring onions, finely chopped
½ quantity Cheese Sauce, see page 23
30 g (1 oz/¼ cup) grated Cheddar cheese
spring onion, to garnish

Preheat oven to 160C (325F/Gas 3). In a bowl, beat egg yolks with salt and pepper to taste. In a separate bowl, whisk whites to stiff peaks and fold into egg mixture.

Melt butter in a 20 cm (8 in) omelette pan with an ovenproof handle. Pour in egg mixture, spreading lightly, and cook for 1 minute.

Sprinkle omelette with onions, then transfer to oven and cook for 5 minutes, until half set. Quickly spoon on cheese sauce and sprinkle with cheese. Return to oven and continue cooking for 5 minutes, until set. Do not fold this omelette but, instead garnish with a spring onion and serve the omelette cut in half. Serve at once.

Serves 2.

— FLUFFY CHICKEN OMELETTE —

5 eggs, separated
salt and pepper
2 teaspoons chopped fresh parsley
30 g (1 oz/6 teaspoons) butter
125 g (4 oz) cold cooked chicken, diced
1 tomato, skinned and sliced
fresh parsley sprigs, to garnish

Preheat oven to 160C (325F/Gas 3). In a bowl, beat egg yolks with salt and pepper to taste and stir in chopped parsley. In a separate bowl, whisk whites to stiff peaks and fold into the egg yolk mixture, using a large metal spoon.

Melt butter in a 20 cm (8 in) omelette pan with an ovenproof handle. Pour in egg mixture and cook for 1 minute.

Sprinkle on diced chicken, transfer to oven and cook for 5 minutes, until half set. Put tomato slices over half the omelette, fold over and continue cooking for 5 minutes, until set. Garnish with fresh parsley sprigs and serve at once.

Serves 2.

PRAWN OMELETTE

60 g (2 oz/¼ cup) butter

60 g (2 oz) mushrooms, thinly sliced

15 g (½ oz/6 teaspoons) plain flour

155 ml (5 fl oz/⅔ cup) milk

125 g (4 oz) peeled cooked prawns, thawed if frozen

salt and pepper

5 eggs

whole chives, to garnish

Preheat oven to 160C (325F/Gas 3). Melt half butter in a small saucepan, add mushrooms and cook for 1 minute. Stir in flour and cook for 30 seconds, then gradually stir in milk and bring to the boil. Stir in prawns and season to taste with salt and pepper. Remove from heat.

In a bowl, beat eggs with salt and pepper. Melt remaining butter in a 20 cm (8 in) omelette pan with an ovenproof handle, pour in egg mixture and cook for 1 minute. Transfer to oven and cook for 5 minutes, until half set. Spoon over prawn mixture and continue cooking for 5 minutes, until set. Do not fold this omelette, but, instead, serve cut into pieces. Garnish with chives and serve at once.

Serves 2.

Variation: Add 60 g (2 oz) cooked mussels to the prawn and mushroom mixture, if desired.

OMELETTE LORRAINE

125 g (4 oz) uncooked ham or gammon steak, diced

60 g (2 oz/¼ cup) butter

6 eggs

salt and pepper

60 g (2 oz/½ cup) grated Gruyère cheese

1 teaspoon chopped fresh chives

Preheat oven to 160C (325F/Gas 3). Put ham and half the butter into a 20 cm (8 in) omelette pan with an ovenproof handle and cook over low heat until ham is cooked through.

In a bowl, beat eggs with salt and pepper to taste, then stir in cheese and chives. Add remaining butter to pan, pour egg mixture over ham and cook for 1 minute. Transfer to oven and cook for 10 minutes, until set. Do not fold but, instead, serve cut in half. Serve at once.

Serves 2.

Variation: Use thinly sliced prosciutto instead of uncooked ham or gammon and omit cooking.

RUSSIAN OMELETTE

250 ml (8 fl oz/1 cup) single (light) cream
90 g (3 oz/¾ cup) plain flour
6 eggs
salt and pepper
125 g (4 oz/½ cup) butter
60 g (2 oz) smoked salmon, cut into strips
lemon slice, smoked salmon cone filled with caviar or lumpfish roe and fresh dill sprig, to garnish

Preheat oven to 200C (400F/Gas 6). In a bowl, beat cream and flour until smooth, then add eggs, one at a time, beating well after each addition. Season well with salt and pepper and beat until creamy.

Melt butter in a 20 cm (8 in) omelette pan with an ovenproof handle over low heat, pour in batter and cook for 2 minutes. Transfer to oven and cook for 8 minutes, until set. Cover with smoked salmon and serve at once. Do not fold this omelette but, instead, serve cut into pieces. Garnish with a lemon slice, smoked salmon cone filled with caviar or lumpfish roe and fresh dill sprig and serve at once.

Serves 3.

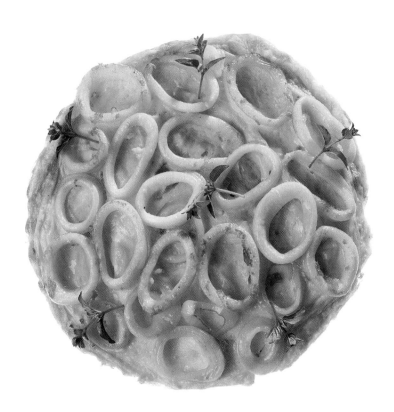

— ITALIAN SQUID OMELETTE —

250 g (8 oz) fresh squid
9 teaspoons vegetable oil
1 clove garlic, crushed
6 eggs
salt and pepper
30 g (1 oz/6 teaspoons) butter
fresh marjoram sprigs, to garnish

Preheat oven to 160C (325F/Gas 3). To prepare squid, pull off tentacles, removing stomach and ink bag with them, then wash body of squid and peel off skin. Cut beak and ink bag from tentacles and discard. Wash body and tentacles well and drop into a saucepan of boiling water. Bring back to the boil, drain and rinse body and tentacles in cold water, then slice into rings.

Heat oil with garlic in a 20 cm (8 in) omelette pan with an ovenproof handle. Add squid and fry for 3 minutes, stirring occasionally.

Meanwhile, in a bowl, beat eggs with salt and pepper to taste. Drain oil from pan and add butter. Pour egg mixture into pan and cook for 1 minute, then transfer to oven and cook for 10 minutes, until set. Do not fold but, instead, serve cut into quarters. Garnish with marjoram and serve at once.

Serves 4.

HALF MOON OMELETTES

4 eggs
salt and pepper
125 g (4 oz) peeled cooked prawns, thawed if frozen and finely chopped
3 teaspoons light soy sauce
3 teaspoons dry sherry
1 teaspoon sugar
$\frac{1}{2}$ teaspoon salt
30 g (1 oz/6 teaspoons) butter
vegetable oil for cooking
250 g (8 oz) cooked spinach or peas
155 ml (5 fl oz/$\frac{2}{3}$ cup) hot chicken stock
peeled prawns, to garnish

In a bowl, beat eggs with salt and pepper to taste. Prepare filling by putting prawns, soy sauce, sherry, sugar, salt and butter into a saucepan and tossing over low heat for 3 minutes.

Brush a 10 cm (4 in) omelette pan with a little oil and pour in 3 teaspoons of the egg mixture. Put 2 teaspoons prawn filling on one side of egg, fold over and press edges gently to seal. Turn omelette with a palette knife and cook for 20 seconds, until set. Continue until all the eggs and filling are used.

Oil a large frying pan and add cooked spinach or peas. Place all the omelettes on top in a single layer, pour over hot stock, cover and simmer over low heat for 5 minutes. Serve omelettes in bowls with broth and peas, garnished with peeled prawns. This is an ideal first course for a Chinese meal.

Serves 4.

Note: Tiny shrimps, smaller than prawns, are available from some supermarkets and Chinese grocery stores. They can be left whole for this recipe.

EGG FOO YUNG

4 eggs
3 teaspoons light soy sauce
½ teaspoon salt
3 teaspoons vegetable oil
60 g (2 oz) cooked ham, shredded
90 g (3 oz) bean sprouts
4 spring onions, finely chopped
spring onion brush, to garnish

In a bowl, beat eggs with soy sauce
and salt. Heat a 17.5 cm (7 in)
omelette pan, add oil, then ham,
bean sprouts and onions and cook
for 2 minutes, stirring well.

Pour in eggs and stir with a fork
until mixture has just set. Put under
a hot grill for 1 minute, until
golden-brown. Garnish with a spring
onion brush and serve at once.

Serves 2.

—— CAVIAR OMELETTES ——

6 eggs
salt and pepper
30 g (1 oz/6 teaspoons) butter
60 g (2 oz) caviar
155 ml (5 fl oz/⅔ cup) thick sour cream
fresh coriander sprigs, to garnish

In a bowl, beat eggs with salt and pepper to taste. Melt a little butter in a 17.5 cm (7 in) omelette pan, put in 6 teaspoons egg mixture and cook until just set. Lift onto a baking sheet and keep warm, then repeat until all eggs are used.

Spoon a little caviar on to each miniature omelette and top with sour cream. Fold omelettes over, garnish with coriander and serve at once. If preferred, the omelettes may be left until cold before filling and serving.

Serves 4.

– PERSIAN WALNUT OMELETTE –

6 eggs
90 g (3 oz/¾ cup) walnuts, finely chopped
60 g (2 oz/⅓ cup) currants
4 tablespoons fresh white breadcrumbs
6 teaspoons chopped fresh chives
¼ teaspoon turmeric
salt and pepper
30 g (1 oz/6 teaspoons) butter
chopped walnuts and fresh mint sprigs, to garnish

In a bowl, beat the eggs, then fold in walnuts, currants, breadcrumbs, chives, turmeric and salt and pepper to taste.

Melt butter in an omelette pan, pour in egg mixture and cook over low heat until set. Put under a hot grill for 1 minute, until golden-brown. Cut into quarters, garnish with walnuts and mint and serve at once.

Serves 4.

- ITALIAN COUNTRY FRITTATA -

1 courgette (zucchini), diced
1 stick celery, diced
60 ml (2 fl oz/¼ cup) vegetable oil
2 tomatoes, skinned, seeded and chopped
salt and pepper
4 eggs
2 tablespoons grated Parmesan cheese
1 teaspoon chopped fresh basil
extra Parmesan cheese for sprinkling
fresh mint sprigs, to garnish

Put courgette (zucchini) and celery into a large frying pan with half the oil and cook gently over low heat for 5 minutes. Add tomatoes and salt and pepper and simmer for a further 15 minutes, stirring occasionally.

In a bowl, beat eggs with cheese and basil. Add remaining oil to pan and heat for 1 minute, then pour in egg mixture and cook for 4 minutes over low heat. Carefully turn mixture and continue cooking other side for 4 minutes. Cut into quarters and sprinkle with Parmesan cheese. Garnish with fresh mint sprigs and serve at once.

Serves 4.

— FRENCH PICNIC OMELETTE —

3 eggs
salt and pepper
60 g (2 oz/¼ cup) butter
1 small French loaf
8 slices salami
3 tomatoes, sliced
watercress sprigs

In a bowl, beat eggs with 3 teaspoons water and salt and pepper. Melt half the butter in a 17.5 cm (7 in) omelette pan over low heat, then turn up heat and pour in eggs. Draw mixture from sides to middle of pan, allowing uncooked egg to set quickly, repeating until all egg mixture is lightly cooked.

Split bread in half lengthways and lightly spread surface with remaining butter. Fold over one-third omelette away from handle of pan.

Remove from heat and hold handle of pan with palm uppermost and turn omelette on to half the bread. Top with slices of salami and tomato and watercress sprigs. Cover with remaining bread. To carry on a picnic, wrap in foil, then cut into slices to serve.

Serves 4.

SPANISH OMELETTE

2 large tomatoes, skinned and chopped

1 small onion, finely chopped

1 small green pepper (capsicum), cored, seeded and finely chopped

1 thick slice cooked ham, diced

1 cooked potato, diced

1 clove garlic, crushed

3 teaspoons olive oil

4 stuffed green olives, sliced

4 eggs

salt and pepper

Put tomatoes, onion, pepper (capsicum), ham, potato and garlic into a large frying pan with oil. Cook over low heat, stirring often, for 7–8 minutes, then stir in olives.

In a bowl, beat eggs with salt and pepper to taste. Pour over vegetables and cook quickly over high heat for 3 minutes. Put under a hot grill for 1 minute until golden. Serve at once.

Serves 2.

OMELETTE CON CARNE

250 g (8 oz) cooked beef, minced
3 teaspoons oil
440 g (14 oz) can tomatoes
½ teaspoon Tabasco sauce
1 small green pepper (capsicum), cored, seeded and cut into strips
salt
6 eggs, separated
9 teaspoons tomato juice
pepper
30 g (1 oz/6 teaspoons) butter
strips of green pepper (capsicum) and corn chips, to garnish

Put the meat and oil into a saucepan and stir over low heat until lightly browned. Add tomatoes and their juice, Tabasco sauce and pepper (capsicum) and simmer over low heat for 20 minutes, stirring often. Season to taste with salt.

In a bowl, beat the egg yolks until thick and pale. Fold in the tomato juice and salt and pepper. Whisk egg whites to stiff peaks and fold into egg yolks.

Melt butter in a 17.5 cm (7 in) omelette pan, pour in egg mixture and cook until fluffy and just set. Put under medium grill for 1 minute, until golden. Lift on to serving plate with a palette knife and spoon over meat sauce. Garnish with pepper (capsicum) strips and corn chips. Serve at once, cut into pieces.

Serves 2–3.

PIPÉRADE

60 g (2 oz/¼ cup) butter
1 large onion, finely sliced
2 green peppers (capsicums), cored, seeded and cut into strips
1 garlic clove, crushed
500 g (1 lb) tomatoes, skinned and finely chopped
salt and pepper
6 eggs
125 g (4 oz) bacon rashers, rinds removed
fresh parsley sprig, to garnish

Melt butter in a large frying pan and cook the onion over low heat for 5 minutes, until softened. Add peppers (capsicums) to the pan with the garlic and gently cook for 5 minutes.

Add tomatoes and salt and pepper to taste and cook, covered, for 20 minutes, stirring occasionally.

In a bowl, beat eggs lightly. Uncover tomato mixture, pour on eggs and cook over low heat, lifting eggs constantly with a fork.

While eggs are cooking, grill bacon rashers until just crisp. Drain well on absorbent kitchen paper. When eggs are just set, lift onto a warm flat serving dish and cover with grilled bacon rashers. Garnish with fresh parsley sprigs and serve at once, cut into quarters.

Serves 4.

— ITALIAN PIZZA OMELETTE —

3 teaspoons vegetable oil
1 small onion, finely chopped
220 g (7 oz) can tomatoes
60 g (2 oz) button mushrooms, thinly sliced
pinch of dried marjoram
salt and pepper
two 3-egg Basic Omelettes, see page 76
30 g (1 oz) Mozzarella cheese, thinly sliced
1 tomato, sliced
4 thin slices salami, halved
fresh marjoram sprigs and few capers, to garnish, if desired

Prepare the topping before making the omelettes. Heat the oil in a small saucepan and fry the onion over low heat for 3 minutes, then add tomatoes and their juice, mushrooms, majoram and salt and pepper to taste. Simmer, uncovered, for 10 minutes, until mixture is reduced by half.

Prepare the omelettes and when two-thirds cooked, spoon half the tomato mixture over each one.

Arrange cheese and tomatoes on top, then put under medium grill to set omelettes and melt cheese. Roll salami slices into cones and place 4 on each omelette. Garnish with marjoram and capers, if desired, and serve at once.

Serves 2.

INDEX